CONRAD: A REASSESSMENT

CONRAD

A Reassessment

DOUGLAS HEWITT

ROWMAN AND LITTLEFIELD

TOTOWA, NEW JERSEY

TO

HJÖRDIS AND PAUL ROUBICZEK

© This Edition 1975 Douglas Hewitt

This Edition published in the United States 1975
by ROWMAN AND LITTLEFIELD, Totowa, N.J.

First published 1952
Third edition 1975

Library of Congress Cataloging in Publication Data

Hewitt, Douglas John, 1920–
    Conrad; a reassessment.

    Includes bibliographical references.
    1. Conrad, Joseph, 1857-1924.   1. Title.
PR6005.04Z744 1975   823'.9'12   74-19449
ISBN 0-87471-600-4

Printed in Great Britain

CONTENTS

PREFACE TO THE THIRD EDITION

It is an experience both comic and disconcerting to find oneself labelled, as has happened to me in several books on Conrad, as one of the founders of a school—in this case the Achievement-and-Decline school of Conrad criticism. I do not want to disclaim my share of paternity, for it does indeed seem to me that Conrad's best work was done in the first half of his career and that thereafter, with certain remissions (most notably *The Shadow Line*), his work declined. But, thinking about why it seemed important to point to a decline, I am very aware that my aim was thus to emphasise the nature of his achievement. The decline and the possible reasons for it are not—to me, at any rate—very interesting in themselves. They seemed important at the time when I was writing because I thought that Conrad was often mis-understood, that he often appeared to misunderstand in retrospect what was valuable in his own work, and that it was necessary, therefore, to free our view of him both from many of his own comments and also from inferior works which might hamper a just appreciation of his great novels and stories. This does not seem much of a danger now, though to contrast the good and the bad remains a useful way of defining the nature of the good.

When preparing the second edition I was aware of other dangers, particularly of the tendency on the part of some critics to extract from the works symbolic schemes, frequently of a highly specious nature, at the expense of the actual. Now that a third edition is called for I am glad to continue the argument and to take issue with what I believe to be another misconception—that Conrad is best talked about as a systematic metaphysical thinker. I have accord-ingly replaced my previous 'Conclusion' with a new one in which I try to define more clearly his true achievement.

Oxford, 1975

PREFACE TO THE SECOND EDITION

The title of this book is out of date. Conrad's reputation when it was published in 1952 was very different from what it has now become. I could say in my 'Introduction' that 'his true significance is now beginning to be appreciated,' but he was still very frequently discussed as a writer of sea-stories, an essentially Romantic spinner of yarns about adventures in exotic latitudes, a novelist of limited scope and limited, if real, value. A number of critics had written perceptively about him—notably Muriel Bradbrook, F. R. Leavis, M. D. Zabel and A. J. Guerard—, though it seems to me typical of the changed situation that, while now we have bibliographies and checklists in plenty, then I never discovered the best criticism, Guerard's 1947 New Directions pamphlet, until after my book was in print. It still seemed necessary to proclaim him as a major novelist and it did not surprise me that even a very sympathetic reviewer in the *Times Literary Supplement* judged that I was 'too exuberant' in suggesting that few English novels do not look superficial in comparison with Conrad's best work. The tone of present critical discussion suggests that my exuberance has become orthodox.

My aim in writing the book was not only to assert Conrad's stature but also to try to discriminate between his works, which seemed to me then to be lumped promiscuously together, so that *Nostromo*, say, and *Chance* were often considered as of about the same importance. Here, again, the situation has changed. I could no longer say of 'The Secret Sharer' that 'its extraordinary virtues have attracted surprisingly little attention', nor could Guerard say, as he did in 1947, 'The story is so little known that a brief summary may be of use.' There is now general agreement about the relative importance of Conrad's works and there is a whole textbook devoted to 'The Secret Sharer'.

The reasons for this change are worth a little thought and so is the question whether we should feel totally happy about so sweeping a victory for judgments which, comparatively recently, appeared to be those of a minority.

In speaking thus of victory it is as well to be clear what we are talking about. Conrad has become established as a modern classic, a writer who is widely studied, examined, written about and researched into. What is not so clear is whether he is widely read with appreciation and pleasure. I have the impression that his apparently unchallengeable status among the critics has not been accompanied by a comparable popularity with the common reader. This is an impressionistic judgment, for figures upon which to base it would be hard to come by; the common reader is an elusive being. But if it is true the victory would be rather hollow and the critics ought to feel disappointed.

There are certainly plenty of them. Professor Guerard commented in the Preface to his *Conrad the Novelist* that 'it is safe to say that in 1947 the large majority of critics in America did not read Conrad at all.' By 1960, F. R. Karl could say in *A Reader's Guide to Joseph Conrad:* 'In the 1950's, the centennial anniversary of his birth has increased the flow of Conrad studies, until, next to Joyce and perhaps Faulkner, he is at present the most discussed of any modern author writing in English.' This change of estimation is true for England as well as America, though the flow of publication has been much smaller. In 1948, when I wrote the article, published in *The Cambridge Journal,* upon which this book was based, I found to help me only a number of memoirs of Conrad, some collections of his letters, the biographical writing of Aubry, which we now know to be unreliable (I said that Conrad edited his recollections but I had no idea how far the editing went), half a dozen or so critical studies and a scattering of articles. Now we have the excellent biography by Jocelyn Baines, more collections of letters (for some of which we are indebted to such Polish and Polish-

American scholars as Zdzislaw Najder), numerous detailed studies of those periods in his life from which he drew the raw material for his works—most notably his time as a seaman; above all, critical and interpretative books and articles have multiplied exceedingly. The 'Selected Check-list' in the 1964 Conrad Number of *Modern Fiction Studies*, for example, lists some ninety items under the heading 'Heart of Darkness', sixty-seven of them dating from the preceding dozen years. Conrad, in short, is now part of the academic critical industry.

For this there are many reasons. Most good writers suffer a decline in reputation in the generation after their deaths. The public which they have won during their lives is dying off and their children's teeth are set on edge. A generation or so later the writer is rediscovered; frequently, as has been the case with Conrad, this rediscovery involves a consider-able reassessment of which of his works are the significant ones. Moreover, the general development of criticism has been favourable to an interest in Conrad. The study of fiction in the past twenty years has exploited the methods which were earlier developed in criticism of poetry and poetic drama; formal analysis has dominated much thinking, attention has been shifted from plot to symbolic pattern, from the documentary aspect of novels to the concept of long works as sustained metaphors. Our reading of many writers has been affected by this—Dickens is an obvious enough example of a beneficiary of this approach. Conrad, with his great attention to structure, to pattern and to symbol, is obviously attractive to any critic who wishes to exploit the resources of this method.

Inevitably, we ask whether there is really all that much to say about Conrad—whether there is really all that much to say about any writer (are there any literary critics who do not sometimes suffer from grave misgivings about literary criticism as such?). But I was fortunate; fairly soon after coming down from Cambridge, where, so far as I can remember, I never heard his name mentioned, I became interested in Conrad and found I wanted to discuss and elucidate his works. I enjoyed myself when what has turned out to be a flood of criticism had just started, and it would ill become me to be grudging about the later offerings of those who share my enthusiasm. A great deal of detailed research about Conrad's reading, of scholarly investigation into his 'sources' is bound to be wasted effort; but some valuable lines of thought have been opened up. A great deal of highly detailed criticism of his work is bound to turn into the implausible extraction of more and more meaning from smaller and smaller passages; but some valuable insights have been achieved.

What does make me uneasy is the triumphant growth of certain assumptions about the nature of Conrad's art which, in this book, I may seem to be proclaiming. I can express this best—if, perhaps, with an element of parody—by saying that the way in which Conrad was once commonly talked about led me to protest against a view which seemed too narrow because it conceived the telegraph wire in *Nostromo*, say, as only a means of conveying messages which might advance a plot about revolution and civil war. The way in which he is talked about now more often makes me want to protest against a narrowness which sees it only as a symbolic umbilical cord linking the womb-like mine with the town which has metaphorically issued from it but which, nevertheless, by the strange logic of archetypes, rests by the amniotic waters of mother sea.

There is a tendency which, given the present temper and organisation of English studies, seems virtually inevitable, to search for 'interpretations' which allow the critic to participate in a quasi-creative process of discovery. The first readers of major novels enjoy this pleasure quite naturally and so do those who, later, read them intelligently quite outside the academic environment. But the obvious way for later professional critics to obtain these joys is to present radical reinterpretations. Conrad has had his share of these. Some, in their search for originality, strain credulity beyond breaking point and, like all our mistaken exercises in ingenuity, can safely be left to oblivion. But there is one general tendency which seems an orthodoxy among a substantial number of Conrad's recent critics, and this deserves attention. Its nature is best made clear by a few rather typical quotations from a number of books which I have read in the line of duty in the past two or three years:

'At this point in the narrative, Conrad shifts the imagery to a mythic referent. Marlow is transformed from the captain of a river steamer into a hero who has as his mission the simultaneous discovery of his own destiny and a beneficent talisman which will work for the good of all mankind.'
(Ted E. Boyle: *Symbol and Meaning in the Fiction of Joseph Conrad.* 1965)

'The Christian symbolism is boldly announced with the name of Heyst. However it might be pronounced in Swedish, it is certainly rhymed with Christ by an English-speaking reader.'
(Charles Child Walcutt: *Man's Changing Mask.* 1966)

' "Heart of Darkness," then, as the account of a journey into the center of things —of Africa, of Kurtz, of Marlow, and of human existence—poses itself as the refutation of such a journey and as the refutation of the general, metaphorical conception that meaning may be found within, beneath, at the center.'
(James Guetti: *The Limits of Metaphor.* 1967)

'But it is the aquarium image that sounds the tonic chord of this image-sequence, and that simile, which borrows a resonance from the earlier metaphor of the "socially drowned", is linked in a chain of ironic allusions to the Fisheries question that preoccupies Sir Ethelred . . .'
(Donald C. Yelton: *Mimesis and Metaphor.* 1967)

'The man whose capital helps to finance reconstruction, Mr. Holroyd, is a kind of God figure. (The temptation to point out the similarity of Holroyd to Holy rōd is overwhelming).'
(Claire Rosenfield: *Paradise of Snakes.* 1967)

I am not suggesting that these quotations give a complete account of the range of their authors' interests, but I do not think that they misrepresent the bias of their minds, and anyone who keeps abreast of the tide of writing about Conrad must surely acknowledge that they are typical of a prevailing attitude and that it would be easy to duplicate them from other critics.

Such criticism directs attention primarily to the symbolic

rather than the literal sense of Conrad's works; sometimes it brushes aside the literal sense. Usually, in the process of relentless symbolisation one novel is replaced by another.

Frequently an emphasis upon the books as symbolic reticulations is extended to assimilate them to more general symbolic schemes, usually of a Freudian or Jungian kind or some eclectic variant of these systems. A man who writes about what he knows well and who happens to know well the sea, villages surrounded by jungle, rivers, dark-skinned peoples, storms, land-locked harbours and constricted cabins, and whose method of composition relies upon the use of such motifs as the treasure seekers of Azuera and the impenetrable darkness of the African river is obviously a tempting subject for massive reinterpretation. But the function of the symbolic structures of Conrad's works is to reinforce the durability of his created world and to direct our attention within it. All too often this type of criticism reduces the magnificently specific novels to vague, generalised fables, hardly distinguishable from all the other novels which have been subjected to the same treatment.

If, once, it seemed necessary to draw attention to the way in which the journey up the African river is equated with Marlow's journey to the climax of his understanding, it now seems important to say that he went up the river in a steamboat which was used to transport ivory extorted from the native people. If, once, it seemed necessary to elucidate the structural symbolic significance of the silver of the mine in *Nostromo*, it now seems important to emphasise that it is a source of wealth which causes the English and Americans to meddle in what we now call an underdeveloped country. If, once, it seemed necessary to point out how Conrad shows that Gentleman Brown can disarm Lord Jim by appealing to his inner weakness and making him feel an 'unforeseen partnership', it now seems equally necessary to assert that *Lord Jim* is first and foremost a novel about moral dilemmas of a real kind. More important still, I think, would be to show that the moral issues are, at least in part, ones with which Conrad, an ex-seaman, would have been at home, though most of us are not: the relationship between professional judgment (that a man who has failed as a ship's officer cannot again be trusted with responsibility) and human judgment (that none of us can afford to judge another man, that none of us dare).

In short, belief in the greatness of Conrad as a symbolic novelist is now orthodox. There is no longer any pressing need to draw attention to the patterns of his imagery or the symbolic resonances of his scenes. There probably is need to emphasise how rooted in the literal world are those symbolic and metaphorical effects, to emphasise that they are so potent precisely because they mediate a vision of life which is both complex and intense and, as we have had all too much opportunity to observe since his death, disturbingly prophetic. I am thinking especially of his political prescience. *Nostromo* now seems a remarkably central novel. The plight of underdeveloped countries with resources which attract foreign capital, the situation of the more liberal Europeans or Americans who support one section of a country against another and then find that they cannot disown their puppets, the predicament of the 'liberals' among the puppets in the brutality of civil war—the central importance of these themes needs no underlining now. There was a time, a few years ago, when the plot of *Nostromo* seemed to be in the process of re-enactment in the Congo.

Even more disturbingly prophetic is 'Heart of Darkness'. I did not say this when I wrote the book because I thought that the obvious way of saying it might appear too neat a melodramatic flourish. Recent tendencies towards interpretation of the story and of Mr. Kurtz in ways which remove them from the world of action and of politics persuades me that the flourish is needed. Mr. Kurtz is a disturbing figure partly because he is so prophetic of what was to come thirty or forty years after the story was written. Hollow at the core, he has a gift of burning eloquence which fascinates decent, simple men and causes the natives of the land to worship him almost as a god. He leaves behind him as his testament the unfinished report about the ascendancy which Europeans should have over lesser races. Its only practical suggestion is the conclusion—'Exterminate all the brutes!'. When his friends tell Marlow that he would have been successful in politics 'on the popular side' because he 'electrified large meetings' and 'would have been a splendid leader of an extreme party' we can understand why Marlow feels that the ordinary people going about their business in the European capital are fools who are unaware of their danger. We can understand because we have seen a man who electrified large meetings and who is most remembered for his policy of exterminating lesser races. Conrad knew a lot about colonialism—as Avrom Fleishman shows in his valuable study, *Conrad's Politics*: he also knew what politics could become when a suitably charismatic figure found his appointed time.

Thus, re-reading this book in a changed critical climate, I observe that some of what I said is less necessary than it was sixteen years ago, but also that some of my comments need more emphasis and that some things which I took for granted probably need uttering. I also find that the change in the assumptions of criticism have slightly altered my estimate of one of the stories in which I was most interested. 'The Secret Sharer' seemed to me when I wrote—to a considerable extent it still does—a key story. In it Conrad treats his favourite theme of the link between his central character and someone who represents a claim which, reluctantly, he cannot deny. But the 'secret sharer', Leggatt, is rather an embodiment of the captain's unease than a man whom he wishes to despise and reject. Leggatt's criminality is hardly an issue and it is surely a mistake to think of him as standing for possibilities of violence and disorder—or of freedom—which the captain-narrator recognises in himself.

He is rather an objective correlative for the unease itself. One consequence of this is, of course, that the disturbance can be disposed of. When Mr. Kurtz dies, Marlow is left with the feelings which Kurtz has forced on him; when Leggatt goes, the captain's insecurity goes with him.

In a climate of opinion which tended very often to read Conrad's stories as yarns rather than as symbolic fables, this story seemed to me more satisfactory than it does now, when the tendency is to interpret symbolically. I now find, for example, that my statement that 'Leggatt is described as his (the captain's) "double" or his "other self" more than twenty times in the course of the story' has somewhat changed its meaning. When I wrote it I was preoccupied with asserting the need to interpret the yarn into a fable; now that most critics would agree—and many would go much farther in the interpretative process than I would—I find that it suggests a certain heavy-handedness, a laboured emphasis. Instead of drawing attention to what we might overlook, the words underline what we already expect.

I have also come to be aware of other limitations in the story. Now that I am not so busy arguing for a symbolical interpretation, I can see that the symbol has weaknesses, that the literal and the symbolic meanings diverge, as they do not in Conrad's best work. One of these weaknesses is obvious enough—that it is only the brilliance of the conclusion which enables us to accept the notion that moments of insecurity can be disposed of for good; the captain, we might say, should find Leggatt in his cabin when he next goes below. If I am right in suggesting that the story 'might almost be an allegory of Conrad's future development', in the sense that his later work is ruined by his attempt to shed the burden of his pessimism, this weakness underlines the essential inadequacy of the vision of his later novels. A more significant weakness, however, is concerned with the literal level of the story which, when I first wrote, seemed as though it could be taken for granted while our attention was directed towards less obvious matters. The captain disposes of Leggatt by a piece of brilliant, risky, frightening navigation. At the symbolic level this is successful, but I would now want to say that a captain who hazards his ship as a way of dealing with his emotional reaction to the responsibility of his first command is not a captain in whose ship I would want to sail. The brilliance of the navigation produces a reaction of feeling in the crew in his favour—he can afterwards feel at one with his command and, we are presumably meant to assume, with his crew. It is not unduly pedestrian to ask whether some of the crew might have second thoughts.

As for my own second thoughts, they are salutary. They make me aware of my own short-sightedness and my blind spots and they also suggest, more generally, how even our detailed discriminations are affected by current critical assumptions.

Nevertheless, though I would not write it now exactly as I wrote it sixteen years ago, this book still represents—given the reservations I have made—what I feel about Conrad. In republishing it I also reflect that it has the limited virtue of brevity.

It contains a number of factual errors which, though they do not effect my argument, should be corrected. On pages 2 and 91 I followed the common view that Conrad fought a duel in Marseilles and, on page 55, that César Cervoni was drowned. Jocelyn Baines' biography has set us right on these matters: Conrad tried to commit suicide and César Cervoni lived a long life. Never trust the teller and do not trust the tale if it claims to be autobiographical.

Oxford, 1968

CONRAD: A REASSESSMENT

INTRODUCTION

'WHO are those fellows who write in the press? Where do they come from?' This outburst in a letter to John Galsworthy was wrung from Joseph Conrad by criticisms of 'The Secret Sharer', but it epitomizes a constant feeling. In a quieter mood he wrote to Sir Sidney Colvin, on 18 March, 1917:*

> Perhaps you won't find it presumption if, after 22 years of work, I may say that I have not been very well understood. I have been called a writer of the sea, of the tropics, a descriptive writer, a romantic writer—and also a realist.

Few writers indeed have been so often misinterpreted, but it appears that his true significance is now beginning to be appreciated. The various accusations of 'Slavism', 'brutality', 'abnormality', 'excessive realism', of being—in his own words—only a 'writer of sea-stuff'—all these have been disposed of, partly by critics, more, perhaps, by time. We can now safely ask what are the unique and peculiar features of his work without seeming to imply that because he was a Pole writing in English he was in some way a freak, or that because he sometimes writes of jungles and shipwrecks he is different in kind from those novelists who deal with places and events more familiar to most of us.

But there are other dangers. One of his main subjects is guilt, and this can be explained plausibly—and perhaps, from the psychologist's point of view, correctly—in terms of his Polish youth.† Few novelists, in fact, offer such fine material for the psycho-analytical delver: childhood in Poland under the rule of the Tsars, a mother who died in

---

* Conrad's letters have been collected and edited by Georges Jean Aubry in his *Joseph Conrad: Life and Letters*, 1927.

† As in Dr Gustav Morf's *The Polish Heritage of Joseph Conrad*, 1930.

exile and a father who was released dying, abandonment of
his own country at seventeen, gun-running in the Caribbean,
a love affair with the ex-mistress of the pretender to the
Spanish throne and a duel for her at eighteen, a British
Master Mariner's ticket and the legal adoption of a new
nationality at twenty-nine, followed by a career as a writer
in which he returns again and again with loving care to the
incidents of his past life, looking at them from different
angles under more or less thin disguises.

We cannot, perhaps, quarrel with those who choose to
use *Nostromo* or *The Rover* or *The Arrow of Gold* as raw
material for psychological deduction, but we should be
clear that this is not literary criticism. One sufficient proof
of this is that the practitioners of the method do not, by it,
discriminate between the qualities of these novels—the first
almost certainly his masterpiece, the second a novel of little
importance, and the third a work which his admirers do well
to overlook. At the risk of seeming to overstate the case
against psycho-analytical interpretations, it seems worth
while stressing that concentration on the peculiar circumstances of the creator's upbringing can do little to help us to a
fuller appreciation of his work—of those parts of it which are
valid not only for him as an outlet for his private feelings
but for us all.* A central theme of Sophocles is also guilt;
it is to be hoped that a deduced account of his boyhood
from the *Œdipus Tyrannus* will not appear.

An excessive attention to his 'technique' can also be
misleading. Certainly Conrad displays extraordinarily fine
craftsmanship—and by the word 'craftsmanship' I mean his
mastery of multiple narration, shifts in time and viewpoint
and so forth, which can be too easily discussed in isolation
from the total meaning of the work. But he displays them

---

* I have in mind statements like the following from Dr Morf's book: 'The final
destruction of Jim consecrates the author's triumph over the guilt-complex.
Tuan Jim's defeat is Joseph Conrad's victory' (p. 164), or: 'In *Lord Jim*, Joseph
Conrad exteriorized, in a symbolic form, the deepest conflicts that arose from the
dualism Polish-English within himself' (p. 166).

as much in his worst novels and stories as in the best. Such craftsmanship taken by itself seems too unimportant to merit our attention. We need to penetrate to something more fundamental, to discover why, for instance, the complicated presentation of *Nostromo* deepens the meaning of the book while that of *Chance* does not.

He himself drew attention to this aspect of his work; in a letter to Richard Curle, dated 14 July, 1923, we find:

> As a matter of fact, the thought for effects is there all the same (often at the cost of mere directness of narrative), and can be detected in my unconventional grouping and perspective, which is purely temperamental and wherein almost all my 'art' consists. This, I suspect, has been the difficulty the critics felt in classifying it as romantic or realistic. Whereas, as a matter of fact, it is fluid, depending on grouping (sequence) which shifts, and on the changing lights giving varied effects of perspective.

The truth of this is obvious to anyone who has read his books with any care. But the continuation of the letter suggests that he is anxious to emphasize the formal aspect at the expense of others:

> It is in those matters gradually, but never completely, mastered that the history of my books really consists. Of course the plastic matter of this grouping and of those lights has its importance, since without it the actuality of that grouping and that lighting could not be made evident, any more than Marconi's electric waves could be made evident without the sending-out and receiving instruments. In other words, without mankind my art, an infinitesimal thing, could not exist.

The reduction of human relationships and values to transmitting and receiving instruments, were it true, would seem to deprive the works of any great value. But it is not true; in his description of Henry James as 'the historian of fine consciousnesses' Conrad is reflecting his own preoccupations.

Conrad does, indeed, often seem to be unaware of what qualities make him a great novelist. By far the greatest obstacle to a correct assessment of his books lies in the fact that he only achieved an authoritative position after his best work had been done and, I believe, after he had started to suppress those aspects of his sensibility which give value to such works as 'Heart of Darkness', 'Falk', *Nostromo*, *The Secret Agent*, 'The End of the Tether', *Lord Jim*, and 'The Secret Sharer'. It is strange that Conrad, so infuriated by the critics who misunderstood him, should in the latter part of his life have written so much which obscures the valuable qualities of his early works. In particular, he offered in his 'Familiar Preface' to *A Personal Record* the statement which has often been taken as a clue to the interpretation of all his books:

> Those who read me know my conviction that the world, the temporal world, rests on a few very simple ideas: so simple that they must be as old as the hills. It rests, notably, among others, on the idea of Fidelity.

Faith in Fidelity may be the guiding thread which can lead us through *Chance*, or *Victory*, or *The Rover*, but it is soon lost in 'Heart of Darkness' or *Nostromo* and other works of the same period, where he treats of ideas and beliefs which are very far from simple and to which any naïve moralizing is irrelevant. To read them in the light of his later novels, and of his own pronouncements when he had achieved a position of authority as one of the leading novelists of the day, is to miss almost everything which they have to give us.

§

This present study grew very largely from reflection on the marked inferiority of most of Conrad's later works to his earlier ones and on the unhelpfulness of his own comments in prefaces and letters. I was forced to the conclusion that, despite his conscious attention to his craft, he was—particularly after the deterioration set in—far less aware of his real powers than one would expect. If it seems presumptuous to claim to know more about his value than he did himself, I take comfort from a passage in a letter which he wrote to Charles Chassé on 31 January, 1924:

> That is the truth as far as I know. *Mais après tout, vous pouvez avoir raison.* Men have but very little self knowledge, and authors especially are victims of many illusions about themselves.

Reflection also had the happy result of persuading me that his best work is not only very different from his account of it, but also very much better.

Because a development or change is perceptible within his work, I have considered the novels and short stories, with one or two exceptions, in the chronological order of their composition. I have not, however, discussed every single work. Some are omitted because, as he says of *A Set of Six* in a letter to Sir Algernon Methuen of 26 January, 1908, 'they are not studies—they touch no problem. They are just stories in which I've tried my best to be *simply entertaining*'. The books of the early 'Malayan period' are omitted because they are not of much intrinsic interest, and all works after *Victory*, with the exception of *The Shadow Line*, because the criticisms of *Chance* and *Victory* are by implication criticisms of these last works also.

CHAPTER I

'Complete Isolation from all Land Entanglements'

THE settings of Conrad's novels and short stories were what first led to the elementary misunderstanding of his work; he was labelled a writer of adventure stories, 'sea-stuff', set in exotic latitudes—the 'Kipling of the South Seas'. His fury is understandable. But the difference between his settings and those of most novelists before him is important because it is not a mere matter of his choosing unusual scenes. His choice is determined by his aims, by the nature of his interest in human nature and moral problems, and we find a clue to the reason for this in a letter which he wrote to Henry S. Canby on 7 April, 1924:

> *Youth* has been called a fine sea-story. Is it? Well, I won't bore you with a discussion of fundamentals. But surely those stories of mine where the sea enters can be looked at from another angle. In the *Nigger* I give the psychology of a group of men and render certain aspects of nature. But the problem that faces them is not a problem of the sea, it is merely a problem that has risen on board a ship where the conditions of complete isolation from all land entanglements make it stand out with a particular force and colouring.

Though, as I have suggested, Conrad often seems to misunderstand the nature of the issues with which his early work deals, his more specifically technical comments are far more acute and reliable; here he puts his finger on the vital point—that it is not the setting itself, but the isolation which it gives that is significant. Such isolation could obviously be attained in circumstances more familiar to the general reader—and Conrad did not, in fact, confine himself to the tropics and the ocean—but, as he once said, he was not good at making up a 'consistent lie'; he was usually stirred into creative activity by recollections of

6

things which he had seen, or done, or been told, and it was on this accumulation of memory that he worked after he had left the sea and settled as a professional novelist. He did not write about the Belgian Congo or the China Seas because he believed that human nature is different there from what it is in London or Paris, but because these were places that he knew and because they enabled him to isolate his characters so that their problems would 'stand out with particular force'. When he chooses to set *The Secret Agent* in Soho, he finds the same passions at work as when he deals with Borneo or an invented South American republic.

This kind of 'particular force' is strikingly different from the effect at which most of Conrad's predecessors were aiming. Their intention is extensive rather than intensive; it is to show the interaction of the individual with the whole of the society in which he lives, to give us—by description or implication—a sense of how vast and multifarious is the world with which he deals. The most extreme pursuit of this comprehensive aim is in the *Comédie Humaine* of Balzac. As we read the great bulk of that series of novels the individuals recede into the background of our view; Cousin Pons and Lucien de Rubempré, Cousine Bette and César Birotteau, though they may often give their names as titles to individual books, become subordinated to his great theme —chaotic French society in all its manifestations and, above all, the Paris of Louis-Philippe.

Other novelists, however, even if they do not announce with Balzac that their aim is to be the 'natural historian of society', are almost as preoccupied with the task. Panoramic views, such as those of *War and Peace*, *Vanity Fair* and *Middlemarch* (whose sub-title is significantly *A Study of Provincial Life*) are common, and even in works where the choice of subject matter is ostensibly narrower we constantly find deliberate implications of the activities of society outside the scope of the story presented to us.

These works often have, in the sense in which Aristotle uses the terms, no beginning and, in particular, no end—nothing 'which is naturally after something else, either as its necessary or usual consequent, and with nothing else after it'; for their full effect, indeed, we must be made to feel that there is a lot else after the last page. In the opening words of George Eliot's 'Finale' to *Middlemarch*: 'Every limit is a beginning as well as an ending'. It is essential, for example, for the force of *War and Peace*, that we should feel that the younger generation who are growing up at the end of the book will have lives with which Tolstoy has chosen not to deal. We are constantly reminded that the novelist has chosen to depict a particular slice of life, but that the rest of life, though uninspected, remains. Characters make their appearance within the plot, coming from parts of society with which the writer is not dealing, appearing—as it is made to seem—accidentally, disappearing again to carry on the life which is outside the range of the present selection, but the implication of whose existence is necessary for the total effect of the book. Even when the main character is in a position of physical isolation (as is Julien Sorel during his long sojourn in the seminary in *Le Rouge et le Noir*), we are reminded from time to time that life is going on outside—life of which we are given only a few hints, but of which we are meant to be conscious as just as full and just as potentially interesting as the point on which our eyes are fixed.

Conrad, on the contrary, sets his scene so that our eyes are never directed outwards to any other part of human society. Most extremely, his setting is the ship, free from 'all land entanglements'. In *The Nigger of the 'Narcissus'*, 'The End of the Tether,' 'The Secret Sharer' and *The Shadow Line* the whole of the vital action takes place in this most extreme form of isolation. But it is just as great, if less obvious, in other works—in the jungle village of Patusan 'within the wall of forests' in the second part of *Lord Jim*, up the African river in 'Heart of Darkness', in the coast province of Sulaco in *Nostromo*. Confined within their walls of forest, or mountain, or sea, the characters of Conrad's books work out the logical consequences of their passions.

In those books where intruders break into the isolation it is notable that they do not come by accident; they belong within the emotional context of the isolated scene. They do not distract or give a new turn to the minds of the main characters; they come in response to a summons or a temptation, to embody aspects of the central situation of the book or to precipitate latent crises.

In *Lord Jim*, for example, Gentleman Brown is no chance arrival; he comes because he has heard of the strange Englishman in Patusan and he brings with him a

> subtle reference to their common blood, an assumption of common experience; a sickening suggestion of common guilt, of secret knowledge that was like a bond of their minds and of their hearts.[1]*

Even in *Nostromo*, the longest and most complex of the works, the emphasis on isolation and on the connection of all the intruders from outside with the situation of the principal characters is just as clear. In the masterly opening of the book Conrad brings us into Sulaco from the sea, and this is appropriate because it is notoriously difficult of access over the mountains. The outside world does not concern itself with the province unless it is invited or tempted to enter. 'I had no notion', the chairman of the railway company says, 'that a place on a sea coast could remain so isolated from the world'.[2] Of the revolution 'they heard only the echoes of these great questions' and 'the very rumours reached it circuitously—from abroad even, so much was it cut off from the rest of the Republic'.[3] In short:

> It had been lying for ages ensconced behind its natural barriers, repelling modern enterprise by the precipices of its mountain range,

---

* Miss M. C. Bradbrook draws attention to this aspect of the book in her study *Joseph Conrad, Poland's English Genius*, 1941, V. *inf.* also, Ch. III.

by its shallow harbour opening into the everlasting calms of a gulf full
of clouds.[4]

When 'modern enterprise' and the troops of Montero do
force the barrier it is because the one is invited by Don
Carlos Gould, the other tempted by the wealth of his silver
mine.

There is, at one time, an isolation within this isolation
when Nostromo and Decoud sail out into the Golfo Placido
in the lighter loaded with silver. Their loneliness is complete: 'Yes', said Decoud, 'Nobody can find us now'.[5]
There is, however, another ship in the gulf which runs them
down; but it is the transport with Sotillo's men from
Esmeralda and it is there because Sotillo is in search of the
silver which the lighter carries.

§

A further and most important difference between the
effect of Conrad's work and that of the other novelists
we have mentioned, follows from this difference of setting
—a difference in the stature of their main characters.

The nineteenth-century novelists, in giving or implying
a view of the whole of a complex society, inevitably show
the comparative unimportance of their main characters,
their insignificance in relation to the hugeness of the life of
a nation or even of a modern city. None of their characters
can ever appear of heroic size. The central figure of a novel
of Balzac, or George Eliot, or Stendhal, or Tolstoy, is the
centre only of the events narrated to us; he is the point upon
which the writer has focused our attention. He is not central
in the sense in which the hero of tragedy is central—in
that the whole of the society depicted is orientated towards
him.

A very common theme of the nineteenth-century novel
is the assault on society by a young man or woman. Becky
Sharp or Julien Sorel or Eugène de Rastignac set out to

make their mark on the world, to establish themselves; but, whether they succeed or fail, the vastness of the 'unconquered' territory is repeatedly emphasized. The young man who is the centre of attention in his provincial town finds that in the capital he is lost in a bewildering complexity of interests, relationships, business and political dealings. However gifted he is, however many people he succeeds in attaching to himself, he will never be the centre. Society will never revolve round him.

Even in a study of a small provincial town like *Middlemarch* and of a character like Dorothea Brooke who in the 'Prelude' is obliquely likened to a cygnet among ducklings, the same effect is apparent. Throughout the first section of the book Dorothea is the centre of attention, with the other personages in varying ways subordinated to her. But within a hundred pages or so, after a discussion by various townsmen on feminine beauty in which Dorothea's lack of charms for some of them is emphasized, we are informed that she is not to Lydgate's taste either, and we move to a study of Lydgate and the Vincy family, for whom Dorothea is merely one among many local figures. She drops out of the story for some time, and however important she may later become to Lydgate and to Rosamond, this is only because of a combination of apparently fortuitous circumstances. She is, in short, the central character of only one of the plots of the novel; in the others she is a minor figure, and for some people of the town it is clear that she has no significance whatever. In such a structure composed of multiple plots— a common form in the nineteenth century—this effect seems inevitable.

Conrad's main characters, on the contrary, are central in the same way as the heroes of tragedy, in that the whole of the isolated 'world' which is presented to us is centred on them and usually dependent, both morally and physically, on them.

In *Lord Jim*, for example, the whole of Patusan is dependent upon Jim; upon his reactions to the inner problems which face him hang the lives and well-being of all the inhabitants. In *The Shadow Line* the narrator emphasizes that everybody on board his ship is looking to him to save them. In 'The Secret Sharer', as the strain of knowing of the presence of his 'other self' tells on the captain, as 'all unconscious alertness' leaves him and he becomes less and less able to command, everybody on board watches his moods because they know that their lives may hang on his decisions.

In the wider scope and more complex structure of *Nostromo* the relationship between the central character and the others is not so simple and direct, but we are left in no doubt that Don Carlos Gould is the 'King of Sulaco'. It is his decision which brings in the 'material interests' to help exploit the mine which Nostromo describes as 'lording it by its vast wealth over the valour, the toil, the fidelity of the poor, over war and peace, over the labours of the town, the sea, and the campo',[6] and it is this action and his support of the Ribierists which cause the invasion of the province by the rebel leaders Montero and Sotillo. Don José Avellanos and his fellow aristocrats may play at politics, at passing resolutions and negotiating with enemies, but Gould is the power behind them; they hang on his lips, and in the crisis he abandons them and makes his own decisions. 'Fussy Joe' Mitchell's description of Mrs. Gould is factually true: 'First lady in Sulaco—far before the President's wife'.

§

It must not be thought, however, that this concentration of attention on figures who are the centres of their isolated 'worlds' is made for the sake of aggrandizing them. There is no question of Lord Jim or Charles Gould's being 'greater' as individuals than Julien Sorel or Dorothea

Brooke. When I speak of the resemblance of Conrad's heroes to those of tragedy I am not suggesting that they are cast in a specially heroic mould. It is the relationship between the main character and his society which is similar, and while this interest in the central and responsible figure no doubt suited well with Conrad's essentially aristocratic and feudal leanings, he does not use this method for the sake of glorifying his heroes. In fact, they are not glorified. But, because they so dominate their surroundings and because there is no interference from outside, their inner problems are mirrored in external events and relationships. The facts of the external world become symbolic of the moral problems with which they are at grips, without ceasing to be facts which are perfectly convincing in naturalistic terms. Thus it is that in some of his works Conrad can make clear and express in terms of actions and of material objects certain moral problems which it might otherwise be difficult to show as other than tenuous, abstract or impossible of definition. It may, indeed, be misleading to speak of 'moral problems' in this way, for we may tend to think of simple questions to which an answer can be found. Often what is asked of the main character is that he should recognize certain qualities in himself and in the world about him. 'Moral and spiritual plight' more nearly expresses the inner situation which is bodied forth in terms of human relationships and physical facts.

This 'externalization' is seen very clearly in *Lord Jim*. The threat to Patusan by Gentleman Brown and his crew of ruffians is the outward form of the threat to Jim's newly gained sense of security by an irruption from his own past. The physical disaster could be avoided if only he could deny the memories which leave him disarmed before Brown's 'reference to their common blood'.

I do not wish to seem to imply that this correspondence between the inner plight of a character and the setting and events of a story is unique, nor that it can only be obtained by this method of isolation. But the degree to which such a unity can be sustained without being grossly and obviously factitious is clearly related directly to the degree to which the story is self-contained. As we have seen, in a typical novel of Conrad the accidental visitor is an impossibility; so, almost, is the accidental object.

In 'The Secret Sharer', for instance, the ladder is not left hanging over the side of the narrator's ship by accident. It is there because his frame of mind when he takes over his first command is one of 'strangeness'; he hopes to over-come the sensation of being, as he says, 'somewhat of a stranger to myself' by staying on deck alone for part of the night, consequently no anchor watch is set and nobody, therefore, hauls the ladder aboard. It becomes the means whereby Leggatt enters the ship and at the same time the means whereby the haunting consciousness of his 'other self' enters the captain's already uneasy mind.*

Thus it is impossible to make any distinction between what is 'natural' and what is 'symbolical' in Conrad's best work; objects which fulfil a symbolical function are not superadded to a story which is complete without them. All the facts of his isolated world play their part in the central character's inner situation and help to make it clear to us. So complete and seemingly inevitable is this 'external-izing' of psychological and moral problems, indeed, that many of Conrad's readers have never realized the existence of the deeper issues. Conrad is outstanding in the extent to which he has always made an appeal at two different levels.

§

Such a method assures great coherence and concentration and the possibility of a powerful expression of the states of

---

* V. *inf.*, Ch. V, pp. 52 and 54–55 for a discussion of the telegraph, the railway and the silver in *Nostromo*, which are potent in the story both as physical facts of the plot and as symbols of the enslavement of the country.

mind of his characters. But clearly it could be used to give force to themes which were at bottom trivial, melodramatic or sentimental. It remains for us to discover the nature of his moral and psychological interests and the importance of the problems with which he deals.

CHAPTER II

'Heart of Darkness'

ONE result of this coherence of Conrad's work is that no paraphrase, no dissecting out of a 'subject', is sufficient to convey the intention and significance of his novels and short stories. The themes are not schematic; they are embodied in the imagery, in the structural pattern, in the minute-by-minute flow of the narration. Nevertheless, after the early 'Malayan' phase of *Almayer's Folly*, *An Outcast of the Islands* and the short stories 'The Lagoon' and 'Karain', he has one recognizable main preoccupation, and it will help to clarify this study if we state it first in general terms, before proceeding to consider individual works in detail. As Conrad himself says in a letter to F. N. Doubleday of 2 June, 1924:

> ... I think that an author who tries to 'explain' is exposing himself to a very great risk—the risk of confessing himself a failure. For a work of art should speak for itself. Yet much could be said on the other side; for it is also clear that a work of art is not a logical demonstration carrying its intention on the face of it.

These books cannot, certainly, be adequately paraphrased; but they can be elucidated and, judging by a good deal of what has been written about them, this elucidation is necessary.

We cannot fail to observe, if we approach Conrad's work without preconceptions, that in almost all his earlier books a penetrating scrutiny is directed against the simple virtues of honesty, courage, pity and fidelity to an unquestioned ideal of conduct. The note is struck as early as *The Nigger of the 'Narcissus'* in the treatment of the sailors' pity for the dying negro, which is seen as 'the latent egoism

16

of tenderness to suffering' which makes them 'highly humanized, tender, complex, excessively decadent'.

In particular we notice the recurrence of one situation which, though it occupies a subordinate place in two or three of the works, dominates many—the situation in which a man who relies on these simple virtues is confronted by a partially apprehended sense of evil against which they seem powerless. The mere realization of the existence of this evil overwhelms him with a sense of insecurity and casts doubt on the supposedly secure foundations of the ideals themselves; the virtues at last become suspect. Moreover, because of the peculiar structure of Conrad's works, the sharp immediacy of the problems which the confrontation raises and the clear knowledge of the significance to others of the main character's actions combine to prevent these realizations from being disregarded as vague self-questionings or moods which can be ignored. This awareness is often brought about through the recognition by the central character of an obscure link between himself and a manifestation of the evil which he cannot fail to know for what it is.

The 'Malayan' stories deal with treachery and cowardice and with the corruption and disintegration of personality which they cause; the theme is widened and deepened in the succeeding works. The standards by which the traitors are condemned are subjected to scrutiny, and it is the resulting sense of insecurity which makes these books so profoundly disturbing.

Since such generalizations, however, mean little on their own, a detailed study of some of the works is necessary, and 'Heart of Darkness' is one of the best for this purpose; it is generally recognized as one of Conrad's masterpieces and the title sounds the note of the dominant imagery of this period.

All commentators have pointed out that this story follows very closely the actual events of Conrad's trip to Stanley

Falls,* but, having noted this, they have generally assumed
that it is to be regarded as a picture of the Dark Continent
and of Mr Kurtz and that the narrator, Marlow, who plays
the part in the book which Conrad played in the actual
journey, is merely the more or less transparent medium
through which we study the exploitation of the Congo
natives and the degradation of Mr Kurtz, the 'hollow
man'. In fact, the story is primarily concerned with the
effect of the country and of Kurtz on Marlow. This is clear
enough from Marlow's own words:

> It was the farthest point of navigation and the culminating point of
> my experience. It seemed somehow to throw a kind of light on
> everything about me—and into my thoughts. It was sombre enough,
> too—and pitiful—not extraordinary in any way—not very clear either.
> No, not very clear. And yet it seemed to throw a kind of light.[7]

The equation between the farthest point of navigation and
the culminating point of Marlow's experience is typical of
Conrad's method. The voyage is both into the impenetrable darkness of Africa and into the darkness of Marlow's
thoughts.

Conrad once said to Edward Garnett: 'Before the Congo
I was just a mere animal', and the reactions of the originally
rather naïve Marlow to his meeting with Kurtz and to the
strange country should hold our attention rather than what
in 'Geography and Some Explorers' [from the volume *Last
Essays*] Conrad describes as: ' . . . the vilest scramble for
loot that ever disfigured the history of human conscience
and geographical exploration'.

One deviation from autobiography is notable. He
changes the facts which would diminish the isolation of
Kurtz's settlement on the river. In 'Geography and Some
Explorers', describing how he 'smoked a pipe of peace at

---

* See 'The Congo Diary' in *Last Essays*. The footnotes of Richard Curle
emphasize how closely Conrad keeps to autobiography. There is, of course, a
certain amount of rearrangement. The exploration party, for instance, arrived in
fact *after* Conrad returned from Stanley Falls.

midnight in the very heart of the African continent, and felt very lonely there', he writes:

> The subdued thundering mutter of the Stanley Falls hung in the heavy night air of the last navigable reach of the Upper Congo, while no more than ten miles away, in Reshid's Camp just above the Falls, the yet unbroken power of the Congo Arabs slumbered uneasily. Their day was over.[8]

In the story, however, Kurz, is alone 'as though he had been an enchanted princess sleeping in a fabulous castle'.[9]

But though Kurtz's position is isolated, Conrad emphasizes from the first that he is not alone in wickedness. Marlow comes on the scene 'after a lot of Indian Ocean, Pacific, China Seas' and we feel him to represent, in his dealings with the Company, all the forces of straightforwardness and honesty. He is confronted by incidents which combine the horrible, the wicked and the farcical as he progresses towards the highest point of navigation on the Congo. (For, though Conrad does not give the river a name, he makes it clear enough by his description—and in a noteworthy image:

> It had become a place of darkness. But there was in it one river especially, a mighty big river, that you could see on the map, resembling an immense snake uncoiled, with its head in the sea, its body at rest curving afar over a vast country, and its tail lost in the depths of the land.[10])

The voyage along the African coast has an air of nightmare —of farcical nightmare.

> We pounded along, stopped, landed soldiers; went on, landed custom-house clerks to levy toll in what looked like a God-forsaken wilderness, with a tin shed and a flag-pole lost in it ... we passed various places—trading places—with names like Gran' Bassam, Little Popo; names that seemed to belong to some sordid farce acted in front of a sinister back-cloth.[11]

He turns for relief to the negroes who paddle out in boats from the shore, men who have 'bone, muscle, a wild vitality, an intense energy of movement, that was as natural and true as the surf along their coast'. He strives to keep his grip on the feelings of sanity and normality to which he has been accustomed. 'For a time', he says, 'I would feel I belonged still to a world of straight-forward facts; but the feeling would not last long'.[12]

They come to an anchored warship, shelling the coast, her men dying of disease:

> In the empty immensity of earth, sky, and water, there she was, incomprehensible, firing into a continent . . . the general sense of vague and oppressive wonder grew upon me. It was like a weary pilgrimage amongst hints for nightmares.[13]

His wonder and disgust at the 'merry dance of death and trade' grows even stronger on shore. There are manacled negroes, negroes worn out and left to die, pointless blastings of a cliff, pointlessly abandoned stores, and stores that seem never to have been intended for any purpose. It is the inefficiency which revolts Marlow as well as the cruelty and the exploitation of the natives. The nightmare has not yet caught him and he rebels. At the Central Station he asserts his difference from the others:

> 'I went to work the next day' [he says] turning, so to speak, my back on that station. In that way only it seemed to me I could keep my hold on the redeeming facts of life.[14]

He can judge and condemn the 'pilgrims' of trade; he understands their plotting, their hopes that the mysterious Mr Kurtz will be dead before the steamboat can reach him; he watches the flaming hut with common-sense detachment, knowing that there is no hope of saving it and confidently superior to the man with the bucket who hopes to extinguish the conflagration—'I noticed there was a hole in the bottom of his pail'. So far, it is important to realize, he has not succumbed to the nightmare. He retains standards by which he criticizes the traders, and the scope of his criticism is wide. He notes with irony the clean collar of the Company's chief accountant:

> His appearance was certainly that of a hairdresser's dummy; but in the great demoralization of the land he kept up his appearance. That's backbone. His starched collars and got-up shirt-fronts were achievements of character. . . . Thus this man had verily accomplished something. And he was devoted to his books, which were in apple-pie order.[15]

He refers again to these books:

> . . . the other, bent over his books, was making correct entries of perfectly correct transactions; and fifty feet below the doorstep I could see the still tree-tops of the grove of death.[16]

He looks back in these passages to the description, at the opening of the story, of the Romans colonizing Britain and to the reflections—at the time apparently approving—on the British devotion to efficiency:

> What saves us is efficiency—the devotion to efficiency . . . The conquest of the earth, which mostly means the taking it away from those who have a different complexion or slightly flatter noses than ourselves, is not a pretty thing when you look into it too much. What redeems it is the idea only. An idea at the back of it; not a sentimental pretence but an idea; and an unselfish belief in the idea. . .[17]

Yet he still pins his own faith to a practical task; the redeeming facts to which he chiefly turns are rivets. Against the 'imbecile rapacity' of the pilgrims he sets the job of getting the ship in order: 'Rivets. To get on with the work—to stop the hole'. His immediate work gains for him the significance of a moral principle. The steamboat, he says,

> rang under my feet like an empty Huntley & Palmer biscuit-tin kicked along a gutter; she was nothing so solid in make, and rather less pretty in shape, but I had expended enough hard work on her to make me love her . . . She had given me a chance to come out a bit—to find out what I could do.[18]

The journey up the river begins to overwhelm him; 'going up that river was like travelling back to the earliest beginnings of the world.' He feels a kinship with the savages who are making an uproar on the banks:

> . . . that was the worst of it [he says]—this suspicion of their not being inhuman. It would come slowly to one . . . what thrilled you was just the thought of their humanity—like yours—the thought of your remote kinship with this wild and passionate uproar.[19]

But he does not go ashore 'for a howl and a dance'. He is too busy with practical tasks, with navigating the boat up the treacherous river, seeing that the boiler continues to work, and looking after the native fireman, so that, as he says: 'neither that fireman nor I had time to peer into our creepy thoughts'.

He comes upon another symbol of practical-mindedness and disinterested devotion to duty in the book abandoned by the pile of firewood—*An Inquiry into some Points of Seamanship*.

> The simple old sailor, with his talk of chains and purchases, made me forget the jungle and the pilgrims in a delicious sensation of having come upon something unmistakably real.[20]

But 'Towson' is only an interlude—a reminder of Marlow's natural seafaring attitude towards life; the book turns out to be the property of the Russian who has given in to Kurtz with 'a sort of eager fatalism'.

In his meeting with Kurtz, Marlow is finally confronted by the heart of darkness; the earlier manifestations of evil, like his touches of fever, are no more than 'playful paw-strokes of the wilderness, the preliminary trifling before the more serious onslaught'.

The choice of the word 'evil' to describe this seems inevitable. I have used the word so far in this study without apology and without explanation. This is not merely because it is the word which Conrad himself so often uses, but because it corresponds to his entire outlook on moral issues. We can discuss many novelists without using this term, speaking of aberrations of conduct, regrettable failings, weaknesses of character and the like, but the most cursory glance at Conrad's work is enough to convince us that he has a conception of a transcendental evil, embodying itself in individuals—a sense of evil just as great as that of any avowedly Catholic or Calvinist writer.

Against Kurtz Marlow cannot defend himself as he can against the pilgrims and the plottings of the other officials. There is something impressive about the man. Marlow is well aware that

> the wilderness had found him out early, and had taken on him a terrible vengeance for the fantastic invasion . . . it had whispered to him things about himself which he did not know, things of which he had no conception till he took counsel with this great solitude—and the whisper had proved irresistibly fascinating. It echoed loudly within him because he was hollow at the core.[21]

Yet he knows that 'he won't be forgotten. Whatever he was, he was not common'.

It is when the manager suggests to Marlow that Kurtz has used an 'unsound method' that we reach one of the most striking and most important phrases of this story—'a choice of nightmares'. We see here that Marlow can no longer defend himself; he can no longer maintain the detachment of a man who relies on standards which are not affected by the corruption and treachery which he meets; he is faced by an experience against which a concern for rivets or for points of seamanship is powerless. He cannot agree, he says, with this formulation of the judgment on Kurtz.

> It seemed to me I had never breathed an atmosphere so vile, and I turned mentally to Kurtz for relief—positively for relief. 'Nevertheless I think Mr Kurtz is a remarkable man', I said with emphasis . . . I found myself lumped along with Kurtz as a partisan of methods for which the time was not ripe: I was unsound! Ah! but it was something to have at least a choice of nightmares.[22]

The phrase recurs when Marlow awakes to find that Kurtz has left the boat to rejoin the savages who have worshipped him as a god, and Marlow's bewilderment at the experience is even more clear:

> The fact is I was completely unnerved by a sheer blank fright, pure abstract terror, unconnected with any distinct shape of physical danger. What made this emotion so overpowering was—how shall I define it?—the moral shock I received, as if something altogether monstrous, intolerable to thought and odious to the soul, had been thrust upon me unexpectedly . . . I left [one of the agents] to his slumbers and leaped ashore. I did not betray Mr Kurtz—it was ordered I should never betray him—it was written I should be loyal to the nightmare of my choice. I was anxious to deal with this shadow by myself alone—and to this day I don't know why I was so jealous of sharing with anyone the peculiar blackness of that experience.[23]

It is useless to ask what is the quality in Kurtz which is absent in the pilgrims. In one sense he is no more than the logical culmination of the hollowness of them all. The difference lies in this—that Marlow can defend himself against the others, he can deny all kinship with them; but just as the manager lumps him along with Kurtz, so he himself feels the link. 'He had kicked himself loose of the earth', Marlow says.

> Confound the man! He had kicked the very earth to pieces. He was alone and I before him did not know whether I stood on the ground or floated in the air.[24]

At the very end of the story he reverts in the most explicit terms to this impotence before Kurtz. He speaks of the illusions of the Intended and says:

> . . . that great and saving illusion that shone with an unearthly glow in the darkness, in the triumphant darkness from which I could not have defended her—from which I could not even defend myself.[25]

It is understandable that he should say that his aunt's attempts to nurse up his strength seemed beside the point, because 'it was my imagination that wanted soothing.'

He accepts the bond established between them, just as he has accepted the bond between himself and the savage clamour from the river bank on the journey upstream. He does not attempt to dissociate himself from the dying man.

> The manager was very placid [he says, describing the return journey] . . . The pilgrims looked upon me with disfavour. I was, so to speak, numbered with the dead. It is strange how I accepted this unforeseen partnership, this choice of nightmares forced upon me in the tenebrous land invaded by these mean and greedy phantoms.[26]

Kurtz dies before they reach the down-river station, and then Marlow is ill and thinks that he will die. It is here that we see most explicitly that his simple ideas of virtue, justice and honour prove inadequate to explain to him the nature of the evil which he has seen and the effect which it has had on him.

> However [he says], as you see, I did not go to join Kurtz there and then. I did not. I remained to dream the nightmare out to the end, and to show my loyalty to Kurtz once more . . . I have wrestled with death. It is the most unexciting contest you can imagine. It takes place in an impalpable greyness, with nothing underfoot, with nothing around, without spectators, without clamour, without glory, without the great desire of victory, without the great fear of defeat, in a sickly atmosphere of tepid scepticism, without much belief in your own right, and still less in that of your adversary. If such is the form of ultimate wisdom, then life is a greater riddle than some of us think it to be. I was within a hair's-breadth of the last opportunity of pronouncement, and I found with humiliation that probably I would have nothing to say. This is the reason why I affirm that Kurtz was a remarkable man. He had something to say. He said it. Since I had peeped over the edge myself, I understand better the meaning of his stare, that could not see the flame of the candle, but was wide enough to embrace the whole universe, piercing enough to penetrate all the hearts that beat in the darkness. He had summed up— he had judged. 'The horror!' He was a remarkable man. . . . And it is not my own extremity I remember best—a vision of greyness without form filled with physical pain, and a careless contempt for the evanescence of all things—even of this pain itself. No! It is his extremity that I seem to have lived through. . . . It was an affirmation, a moral victory paid for by innumerable defeats, by abominable terrors, by abominable satisfactions. But it was a victory. That is why I have remained loyal to Kurtz to the last. . . .[27]

By the end of the story the darkness which exists in the breast of Kurtz and in the dark continent and in the manager and the pilgrims—the darkness from which Marlow cannot dissociate himself—seems to cover the whole world. The inhabitants of the continental capital seem to him to be foolishly unaware of the omnipresent evil.

> Their bearing, which was simply the bearing of commonplace individuals going about their business in the assurance of perfect safety, was offensive to me like the outrageous flauntings of folly in the face of a danger it was unable to comprehend.[28]

The concluding words, in their imagery, extend the sway of darkness:

> Marlow ceased . . . the offing was barred by a black bank of clouds, and the tranquil waterway leading to the uttermost ends of the earth flowed sombre under an overcast sky—seemed to lead into the heart of an immense darkness.[29]

Conrad's mention of how he introduced the word 'silver' into the final paragraph of *Nostromo*, even though he feared that he might spoil it, because the real hero of that book is not the man who gives it its title but the silver itself* is enough indication that 'darkness' is here for some more significant reason than merely that of rounding off the story and putting the reader back into the setting of the storytelling Marlow of later years. We are sent back to the beginning of the story, to the words with which Marlow opens: 'And this also has been one of the dark places of the earth'. We know now that it is still one of them, that what Marlow finds in the heart of the African continent is a darkness which every man may be forced to meet within himself. His faith in fidelity and courage is enough to defend him against the pilgrims and their imbecile rapacity, but it is powerless when confronted by the darkness of Mr

---

* V. *inf.*, p. 54, footnote

Kurtz. We can understand why Conrad said: 'Before the Congo I was just a mere animal'.

§

'Heart of Darkness' is the second in a volume of three short stories. The other two are 'Youth' and 'The End of the Tether', and Conrad once said that he was aware that the three might represent the three ages of man.* 'Youth' we might well describe as the animal state before the experience of the Congo. But it is described by an older man, and behind the eagerness, the voracity of youth we see the waiting shadow. Marlow describes his steering of the small boat towards his first landfall in the East thus:

> I remember the drawn faces, the dejected figures of my two men, and I remember my youth and the feeling that will never come back any more—the feeling that I could last for ever, outlast the sea, the earth, and all men; the deceitful feeling that lures us on to joys, to perils, to love, to vain effort—to death; the triumphant conviction of strength, the heat of life in the handful of dust, the glow in the heart that with every year grows dim, grows cold, grows small, and expires—and expires, too soon, too soon—before life itself.[30]

'Youth' is not merely a story of exciting happenings—a 'good yarn'; it is a celebration of a period of his life by Marlow and it is 'placed' in relation to implications of his later experience. The glamour and enthusiasm are so powerfully conveyed because they have the beauty of threatened things.

The most striking example of this 'placing' is seen in his use of the image of the fire at sea. The description itself is an inevitable anthology piece, but, in the way which is normal in Conrad's work, this is assimilated with the

---

* Letter to F. N. Doubleday, 7 Feb., 1924: '. . . take the volume of *Youth*, which in its component parts presents the three ages of man (for that is what it really is, and I knew very well what I was doing when I wrote 'The End of the Tether' to be the last of that trio)'.

imagery of darkness, omnipresent in this volume, to the
mental state of the narrator:

> Oh, the glamour of youth! [Marlow says] Oh, the fire of it, more
> dazzling than the flames of the burning ship, throwing a magic light
> on the wide earth, leaping audaciously to the sky, presently to be
> quenched by time, more cruel, more pitiless, more bitter than the
> sea—and like the flames of the burning ship surrounded by an im-
> penetrable night.[31]

§

The darkness which attacks Captain Whalley in 'The
End of the Tether' is primarily physical. His only means
of earning money for an unwisely-married daughter is to
act as captain to an unscrupulous owner, and he finds that
he is going blind. He has trusted, in making the contract
which takes no account of the possibility of a breakdown
of his health, on his lifelong freedom from illness, on his
invincible probity, on his great reputation as a seaman. He
is indeed an impressive figure, a survivor from an age of
great sailors in Eastern waters, an embodiment of all the
qualities of the best master mariners:

> broad-chested, without a stoop, as though his big shoulders had never
> felt the burden of loads that must be carried between the cradle and
> the grave . . . with age he had put on flesh a little, had increased his
> girth like an old tree presenting no symptoms of decay . . . conscious
> of his worth, and firm in his rectitude, there had remained to him,
> like the heritage of departed prosperity, the tranquil bearing of a man
> who had proved himself fit in every sort of way for the life of his
> choice.[32]

He has trusted also in the essential goodness of life—'His
feelings had never played him false'[33]; he believes that he
will remain in good health, for 'His Creator knew what use
he was making of his health—how much he wanted it . . .'[34]
He even expresses to Mr van Wyk a simple belief in progress,
a conviction that men had 'progressed . . . in knowledge of
truth, in decency, in justice, in order—in honesty too'.[35]

Firm in the belief that 'On the whole, men were not bad—
they were only silly or unhappy . . . there was not much
real harm in men',[36] he can speak, as we might imagine a
hypothetical honest 'pilgrim' from 'Heart of Darkness'
would speak, of the rôle of the white man in taming the
Malays:

> What men wanted was to be checked by superior intelligence, by
> superior knowledge, by superior force too—yes, by force held in trust
> from God. . .[37]

But the 'visitation' of blindness comes upon him, and he
knows that if he reveals it he will have to wait for the repay-
ment of the money which he has put into the ship. He
conceals it and admits to Mr van Wyk:

> You may have asked me what I had done with my conscience . . .
> I began to tamper with it in my pride. You begin to see a lot of things
> when you are going blind . . . I was not frank with Massy. . . .[38]

He feels the 'humiliation of his falsehood' and Sterne, who,
despite his meanness, is 'really an excellent officer' and who
is alive to the danger of having a captain who cannot
navigate the ship, is shocked when he finds out the truth:
'It was repugnant to his imagination, shocking to his ideas
of honesty, shocking to his conception of mankind'.[39]
Whalley's breakdown is far more than physical. Mr van
Wyk has wondered how far his confidence is merely a
product of his bodily health.

> . . . generally his mind seemed steeped in the serenity of boundless
> trust in a higher power. Mr van Wyk wondered sometimes how
> much of it was due to the splendid vitality of the man, to the bodily
> vigour which seems to impart something of its force to the soul.[40]

Now Whalley feels that:

> He had nothing of his own—even his own past of honour, of truth,
> of just pride, was gone. All his spotless life had fallen into the abyss.[41]

And, just as the peculiar blackness of Marlow's experience
in meeting Kurtz seems 'to throw a kind of light', so

Captain Whalley's blindness lights up the world in which he has so long felt confidence.

> In the steadily darkening universe a sinister clearness fell upon his ideas. In the illuminating moments of suffering he saw life, men, all things, the whole earth with all her burden of created nature, as he had never seen them before.[42]

Marlow is offered only the 'choice of nightmares' and he chooses the 'unforeseen partnership' with Kurtz; Captain Whalley is offered the choice between failing in what he conceives as his duty to his daughter and deceiving Massy in a way which destroys his self-respect and gives him always a 'recrudescence of moral suffering' in his presence. Like Marlow, he finds his assumptions about his moral nature crumbling; his simple faith in unequivocal virtues is shaken by his perception of this darkness.

> The necessity of every moment brought home to Captain Whalley's heart the humiliation of his falsehood. He had drifted into it from paternal love, from incredulity, from boundless trust in divine justice meted out to men's feelings on this earth.[43]

He dies helping Massy to conceal his crime. The ship has been lost because of his devotion to his daughter; his concealment of his blindness has allowed Massy to deflect the compass by putting iron near it and, before going down with the knowledge of the cause of the disaster unrevealed, Captain Whalley places the iron in his own pockets.

CHAPTER III

Lord Jim

Lord Jim was begun immediately after Conrad had finished writing 'Youth' in the summer of 1898, dropped for a time, taken up again after he had written *Heart of Darkness*, and finished in the summer of 1900. 'My first thought', he says in the 'Author's Note' to the Collected Edition, 'was of a short story, concerned only with the pilgrim ship episode; nothing more'. But later he perceived that

> the pilgrim ship episode was a good starting-point for a free and wandering tale; that it was an event, too, which could conceivably colour the whole 'sentiment of existence' in a simple and sensitive character.

Signs of this change in conception may be discerned, though not where we might expect to find them—in a thinness of material or an untidy linking of an illogical second part. Rather are they apparent in a certain muddlement throughout, an uncertainty of the final impression intended by Conrad.

In terms of plot there are undoubtedly two parts to the story: the defection of Jim and the disaster after he seems to have rehabilitated himself; certainly the second part has been added. But, as we have seen,* and as I hope to show here in more detail, they are intimately connected. It is, indeed, difficult to imagine the first part alone as a satisfactory story—certainly as a story by Conrad; the account of a cowardly leap for safety alone could hardly be enough; it demands development.

The general lines of the story are given in miniature in the first chapter. Jim, having developed a romantic view of himself as one who will meet crises with calmness and

* Ch. I, pp. 9 and 13.

determination, is not shaken in this faith by his failure to reach the cutter of his training ship when it puts out to effect a rescue. In the main crisis of the first part of the novel the failure is repeated under circumstances where he offends most unequivocally against 'the obscure body of men held together by a community of inglorious toil and by fidelity to a certain standard of conduct'.[44] His crime is described in terms which are reminiscent of some passages of 'Heart of Darkness'—in terms of what, in that story, is called 'sordid farce'.

> It was part of the burlesque meanness pervading that particular disaster at sea that they did not come to blows. It was all threats, all a terribly effective feint, a sham from beginning to end. . . .[45]

There is a flavour of shameless farce about all the weaknesses and crimes of which Conrad writes at this time; his mean characters are all horribly comic.

Jim's offence is one upon which the Court of Enquiry can have no mercy. But he insists on what, to many of the spectators, seems like trying to brazen it out. Brierly's question: 'Why eat all that dirt?' sums up the feeling of most of them. His hope, however, is that he can rehabilitate himself; as in his first failure in the training ship, he is still sure that at bottom he is ready for any emergency, that he has only been betrayed by circumstances. He will not accept his weakness and stay in a place where men know his story, and so he is driven farther and farther eastwards in the search for a refuge where he can start with a clean sheet and establish himself as a trustworthy man.

Finally, in the jungle settlement of Patusan, he rises to be 'Lord Jim', one whose authority and honour are never questioned and on whom all the natives are dependent. It seems that he has successfully isolated himself from his past, in a place where

> The stream of civilization, as if divided on a headland a hundred miles north of Patusan, branches east and south-west, leaving its

plains and valleys, its old trees and its old mankind, neglected and isolated.[46]

But, despite the fact that he has achieved 'the conquest of love, honour, men's confidence', his past comes in search of him. Gentleman Brown and his crew of cut-throats penetrate the 'wall of forests' which shuts Jim in his isolation. Physically the people of Patusan are more than a match for Brown, but mentally Jim is helpless before this man who combines with his ferocity 'a vehement scorn for mankind at large and for his victims in particular' and who 'would rob a man as if only to demonstrate his poor opinion of the creature'.[47] Everything that Brown says recalls Jim's past weakness, undermines his certainty that he has put behind him a cowardice that was only momentary.

> He asked Jim whether he had nothing fishy in his life to remember that he was so damnedly hard upon a man trying to get out of a deadly hole by the first means that came to hand—and so on and so on. And there ran through the rough talk a vein of subtle reference to their common blood, an assumption of common experience; a sickening suggestion of common guilt, of secret knowledge that was like a bond of their minds and of their hearts.[48]

Jim finds that 'his fate, revolted, was forcing his hand'.[49] We remember the 'unforeseen partnership' with Kurtz which Marlow accepts in 'Heart of Darkness'; but here there is an explicit weakness in Jim to which the partner appeals, and he confronts this appeal under circumstances which make his actions of vital importance for all the inhabitants of Patusan. He speaks no more than the truth when he says: 'I am responsible for every life in the land'.[50] Unable to disown Brown, he brings disaster on the village, takes the death of the chief's son on his own head, and is killed as punishment.

In enlarging the simple story of the pilgrim ship episode, however, Conrad makes a more significant addition than the second half of the story; he introduces Marlow, who, although he does not appear as storyteller until the fifth

D

chapter, is the person to whom we naturally look for commentary and judgment. Judgment we find in plenty—but, far from clarifying the moral issues, Marlow's reflections only succeed in making them more confused.

We remain at the end, I believe, uncertain as to what our verdict on Jim is meant to be. Many views are put before us. The elderly French lieutenant's is clear:

> But the honour—the honour, monsieur! . . . The honour . . . that is real—that is! And what life may be worth when . . . when the honour is gone—*ah ça! par exemple*—I can offer no opinion.[51]

This discourages Marlow; he feels that the lieutenant has 'pricked the bubble'. Yet at times he seems to see Jim as expiating his fault by taking on himself the punishment for the disaster to the village, finally re-establishing his honour. At other times a totally different verdict seems to be presented, as in the conclusion:

> But we can see him, an obscure conqueror of fame, tearing himself out of the arms of a jealous love at the sign, at the call of his exalted egoism. He goes away from a living woman to celebrate his pitiless wedding with a shadowy ideal of conduct.[52]

We remain uncertain whether Jim's moment of panic is one which can be expiated or whether, in the judgment of Marlow the seaman, it has placed him for ever beyond the possibility of forgiveness, uncertain, indeed, whether he is to be blamed for hoping that his weakness can be forgotten or for being so morbidly conscious of it.

The reason for this uncertainty is clear; it is because Marlow, Conrad's mouthpiece, is himself bewildered. As in 'Heart of Darkness', which Conrad wrote while recasting the novel, Marlow plays a greater part than might at first be thought. We may reasonably wonder whether the feelings which brought 'Heart of Darkness' to birth may not be the chief cause why *Lord Jim* developed from a simple short story into a complex novel, for there are many resemblances between the relationship of Marlow and Kurtz and that of Marlow and Jim.

There is an 'unforeseen partnership' not only between Jim and Gentleman Brown but also between Jim and Marlow. 'Why I longed to go grubbing into the deplorable details . . . I can't explain' Marlow says, and wonders:

> Was it for my own sake that I wished to find some shadow of an excuse for that young fellow whom I had never seen before?[53]

A relationship is quickly established between them. When Jim explains his hopes of regaining the respect that he has lost, Marlow says:

> . . . it was I . . . who a moment ago had been so sure of the power of words, and now was afraid to speak, in the same way one dares not move for fear of losing a slippery hold. . . . It was the fear of losing him that kept me silent, for it was borne upon me that should I let him slip away into the darkness I would never forgive myself.[54]

Just as in 'Heart of Darkness' Marlow feels the power of nightmares which his previous experience and standards have not made him ready to understand, so here he is appealed to by Jim in ways for which he is not prepared.

> I was made to look at the convention that lurks in all truth [Marlow says] and on the essential sincerity of falsehood. He appealed to all sides at once—to the side turned perpetually to the light of day, and to that side of us which, like the other hemisphere of the moon, exists stealthily in perpetual darkness, with only a fearful ashy light falling at times on the edge. He swayed me. I own to it, I own up.[55]

It is his own security for which Marlow fears; when he goes for information to one of Jim's fellow officers, it is because he hopes to learn of a redeeming motive for his offence.

> I see well enough now [he says of this incident] that I hoped for the impossible—for the laying of what is the most obstinate ghost of man's creation, of the uneasy doubt uprising like a mist, secret and gnawing like a worm, and more chilling than the certitude of death—the doubt of the sovereign power enthroned in a fixed standard of conduct.[56]

It is obvious enough that Marlow is disturbed because Jim, a fellow English seaman, has not been true to the standards by which they all live.

> I was aggrieved against him [he says], as though he had cheated

me—me!—of a splendid opportunity to keep up the illusion of my beginnings, as though he had robbed our common life of the last spark of its glamour.[57]

But this alone is not sufficient to account for the disturbance of mind in which he is plunged. Jim has also raised doubts of the finality of the very standards themselves; he has suggested the possibility that there are hidden depths of feeling against which they are powerless. Marlow—and, as we shall see in a minute, Brierly—cannot cast Jim out as an offender and forget him, and this is not merely because he is a fellow Englishman, but because he seems to cast doubt on the values by which they could condemn him. Marlow speaks thus of the courage which Jim so signally fails to display:

> ... an unthinking and blessed stiffness before the outward and inward terrors, before the might of nature, and the seductive corruption of men—backed by a faith invulnerable to the strength of facts, to the contagion of examples, to the solicitation of ideas. Hang ideas! They are tramps, vagabonds, knocking at the back-door of your mind, each taking a little of your substance, each carrying away some crumb of that belief in a few simple notions you must cling to if you want to live decently and would like to die easy.[58]

Marlow would seem here to be at one with Winnie Verloc of *The Secret Agent* in her belief that life does not bear looking into very closely, and he continues with the direct implication that such courage is only possible for fools:

> This has nothing to do with Jim, directly; only he was outwardly so typical of that good, stupid kind we like to feel marching right and left of us in life, of the kind that is not disturbed by the vagaries of intelligence and the perversions of—of nerves, let us say.[59]

He goes on to reminisce about 'that good, stupid kind' and about how moved he is when a boy whom he has taken to sea for his first voyage greets him after many years, now grown into one 'fit to live or die as the sea may decree', just as, in the voyage into the heart of darkness, the Marlow of that story clings for a moment to the manual of seamanship as the relief of something tangible in the midst of nightmare. The nostalgia for the normal, for the reliance on simple duties and uncomplicated virtues, is the same, and in both cases the relief can only be temporary.

The feeling of insecurity is deepened by the story of Brierly's suicide. That impeccable captain has felt the same apprehension as Marlow: '. . . the only thing that holds us together', he says, 'is just the name for that kind of decency. Such an affair destroys one's confidence'.[60] We might feel the conclusion to be extreme, for in any group of men there will be some who will betray the faith reposed in them, but we know that, all the time he is enquiring into Jim's case, he is also sitting in judgment on himself and finding a verdict of 'unmitigated guilt'. Marlow speculates that, in his case too, it is the awakening of some idea:

> . . . the matter was no doubt of the gravest import [he says] one of those trifles that awaken ideas—start into life some thought with which a man unused to such a companionship finds it impossible to live.[61]

We are given no hint of what the 'idea' is, except that it is not a commonplace worry about drink, or money, or women, but the effect of what we are told about Brierly is to reinforce Marlow's own obliquely expressed conviction that the virtues of seamanship—all of which Brierly possesses in superabundant measure—are still vulnerable to 'ideas'—that they are not enough in themselves and can easily be imperilled.

For all those issues with which Brierly's virtues can deal, the judgment on Jim is certain, but, in Marlow's words, Jim's attempt to explain his deed gives the impression that

> he was only speaking before me, in a dispute with an invisible personality, an antagonistic and inseparable partner of his existence—another possessor of his soul. These were issues beyond the competency of a court of enquiry.[62]

The effect of muddlement which is so commonly found in *Lord Jim* comes, in short, from this—that Marlow is himself muddled. We look to him for a definite comment, explicit or implicit, on Jim's conduct and he is not able to give it. We are inevitably reminded of the bewilderment with which the Marlow of 'Heart of Darkness' faces Kurtz. By appealing to 'that side of us which, like the other hemisphere of the moon, exists stealthily in perpetual darkness' he confronts Marlow with 'issues beyond the competency of a court of enquiry' and thus shakes the standards by which he would normally be judged.

Here, as in the short story, the experience of Marlow goes far beyond that of the man whom he cannot disown. Kurtz is only a 'hollow man', Jim himself is, by comparison with Marlow, naïve, a romantic thinking in the terms of a boy's adventure story.

But the muddlement goes farther than this. I have so far begged the question by saying 'Marlow, Conrad's mouth-piece'. In fact the confusion seems to extend to Conrad's conception of the story, and this reveals itself in some of the rhetoric given to Marlow. A good deal of this is imprecise and some is little more than a vague and rather pretentious playing with abstractions. It is in these terms that he speaks of the approaching catastrophe:

> *Magna est veritas et . . .* Yes, when it gets a chance. There is a law, no doubt—and likewise a law regulates your luck in the throwing of dice. It is not Justice, the servant of men, but accident, hazard, Fortune—the ally of patient Time—that holds an even and scrupulous balance. . . . Well, let's leave it to chance, whose ally is Time, that cannot be hurried, and whose enemy is Death, that will not wait. [63]

There are many such passages, and they give the impression rather of a man who is ruminating to obscure the issue than of one thinking to clarify it. But they are not 'placed'— Conrad, that is, does not so present them that we see them as deliberate, part of the portrayal of a man who is bewildered. They come rather from his own uncertainty as to the effect at which he is aiming. There is, very clearly, a conflict in his own mind; he raises the issue of the sufficiency of the 'few simple notions you must cling to if you want to live decently', but he does not, throughout the book, face it consistently.

Lord Jim is, at bottom, concerned with the same pre-occupations as 'Heart of Darkness' and other works of this period, but Conrad has chosen to treat them in such a way that he inevitably feels more directly concerned. As he says in the concluding words of the 'Author's Note': 'He was "one of us".' The uncertainty which remains even at the end of the book as to what judgment we should pass on Jim and the passages of imprecise rhetoric are, I believe, an indication that his feelings are too deeply and too personally involved for him to stand above the bewilderment in which he places Marlow. The fixed standards of the simple sailor are those which, above all others, Conrad finds it difficult to treat with detachment. He was too aware of the depths of treachery and cowardice of which men are capable not to cherish whatever seems to provide a defence against them, and at times we have the impression that, just as much as Marlow, he is himself fighting to retain a faith in the efficacy and total goodness of the 'few simple notions'.

CHAPTER IV

'Falk': The Observer and the Dream

IN 'Falk', which was finished in May 1901, Conrad once more tells his story through a narrator who is affected by the experience of the figure who gives his name to the work. The narrator is anxious to have his ship towed out from an unhealthy anchorage* and Falk is of importance to him because he is the only man in the port who has a tug which can do this. The narrator is worried, harassed by financial troubles and by sickness on board his ship, and there is from the start a sense of something uncannily wrong. Falk breaks his agreement to tow him out; he is accused inexplicably of 'very marked want of discretion'; the only possible pilot has been, in effect, bribed by Falk not to help him, and he is involved in 'the wretchedness, the breathlessness, the degradation, the senselessness, the weariness, the ridicule and humiliation' of a fight between the pilot and his guide, the Hussar. He is quite bewildered.

> It was no use fighting against this false fate [he reflects]: I don't know even if I was sure myself where the truth of the matter began. The conviction that it would end disastrously had been driven into me by all the successive shocks my sense of security had received. I began to ascribe an extraordinary potency to agents in themselves powerless.[64]

He feels as if he were under a curse, and can find no reason for it.

> What had I done? [he asks himself]. If I had done something to bring about the situation I should at least have learned not to do it again. But I felt guiltless to the point of imbecility.[65]

When he manages at last to talk to Falk he discovers the

---

* This is an interesting example of Conrad's use of his own experiences. It is treated again from another point of view in *The Shadow Line*.

explanation; he seems to be under a curse because Falk actually is.

Falk appears almost as a force of nature, just as, in the words of the narrator, the girl

> could have stood for an allegoric statue of the Earth. I don't mean the worn-out earth of our possession, but a young Earth, a virginal planet undisturbed by the vision of a future teeming with the monstrous forms of life, clamorous with the cruel battles of hunger and thought.[66]

Centaur-like in his boat, he appears invulnerable.

> We had no quarrel [the narrator says]. Natural forces are not quarrelsome. You can't quarrel with the wind that inconveniences and humiliates you by blowing off your hat in a street full of people. He had no quarrel with me. Neither would a boulder, falling on my head, have had.[67]

There are only two external signs of the curse under which he labours: his habit of shuddering as he draws his hands down his face and his insistence—presented comically as 'peculiar domestic arrangements'—on eating alone. The narrator learns the meaning of these signs and the story of Falk's hunger and cannibalism emphasizes his 'hard, straight masculinity', but in such a way as to undermine our admiration for certain accepted ideals of conduct. When he speaks of the conflict between Falk and the carpenter, the narrator reflects:

> The best man had survived. Both of them had at the beginning just strength enough to stand on their feet, and both had displayed pitiless resolution, endurance, cunning and courage—all the qualities of classic heroism.[68]

The narrator sees Falk as 'a witness to the mighty truth of an unerring and eternal principle' and it falls to him to try to explain this to Hermann, whose daughter Falk wishes to marry. But he can say no more than: 'It is true just as much as you are able to make it; and exactly in the way you like to make it';[69] and 'In these tales . . . there is always a good deal of exaggeration'. For Hermann will never be able to see it as other than a revolting and unjustifiable aberration. Just as the power and impetuosity of the tug reflects Falk's character, so Hermann's is mirrored in his boat:

> The *Diana* of Bremen was a most innocent old ship, and seemed to know nothing of the wicked sea, as there are on shore households that know nothing of the corrupt world. And the sentiments she suggested were unexceptionable and mainly of a domestic order. [70]

and:

> There apparently no whisper of the world's iniquities had ever penetrated. And yet she lived upon the wide sea. . . . She was world proof. Her venerable innocence apparently put a restraint on the roaring lusts of the sea. And yet I have known the sea too long to believe in its respect for decency. An elemental force is ruthlessly frank. [71]

Hermann seems to the narrator not to understand the sea and not to be able to understand the 'simple and elemental desire' of Falk. But he himself can, and it is his reflection which sharpens the point of the story. As he meditates on Falk's revelations his initial feeling of being under an inexplicable curse is transformed into profoundly disturbing reflections on the roots of all our emotions. The hunger which has made Falk eat human flesh is seen as underlying all the refinements of feeling upon which men build up systems of ethics and which they allow to make demands on them.

> He had always wanted to live [he says]. So we all do—but in us the instinct serves a complex conception, and in him this instinct existed alone . . . I think I saw then the obscure beginning, the seed germinating in the soil of an unconscious need, the first shoot of that tree bearing now for a mature mankind the flower and the fruit, the infinite gradation in shades and in flavour of our discriminating love. He was a child. He was as frank as a child, too. He was hungry for the girl, terribly hungry, as he had been terribly hungry for food.
>
> Don't be shocked if I declare that in my belief it was the same need, the same torture. We are in his case allowed to contemplate the foundation of all the emotions—that one joy which is to live, and the one sadness at the root of the innumerable torments. [72]

§

It has often been noted that Conrad seems to be fond of telling his stories through the mouth of a narrator.* But we can see now that it is not enough to regard the captain in 'Falk' or the Marlow of 'Heart of Darkness' and *Lord Jim* as mere story-tellers. What he says in a letter to Sir Sidney Colvin on 18 March, 1917, about his method in *The Shadow Line* is clearly appropriate to these early stories, too: 'My object was to show all the others and the situation through the medium of my own emotions'. The medium of the narrators' emotions is of the first importance; they are deeply concerned in what they see, emotionally involved. The force of the works comes largely from the conflict between what they observe and the standards which they bring to the observation. At bottom the subject of these stories may be said to be the relationship between the observer and the man with whose experience he is confronted.

The danger of discussing Conrad's work in such terms as: 'Why does Conrad often find it necessary to employ a narrator?' lies in the fact that this will tend to make us regard the various storytellers as if they fulfil the same function. Apart from such lay figures as the country doctor Kennedy in 'Amy Foster' and the master-stevedore in 'The Partner', we may distinguish two quite different kinds of narrator. The first is typified by the Marlow of 'Heart of Darkness' and the anonymous narrator of 'Falk', the second by the Marlow of *Chance* and the teacher of languages in *Under Western Eyes*. The Marlow of 1912 is indeed a very different man from the Marlow of 1899. In *Chance* he philosophizes from a position of security and his judgments are accepted at their face-value; in 'Heart of Darkness', as

* E.g. Edward Crankshaw's *Joseph Conrad: Some Aspects of the Art of the Novel*, 1936.

in this whole group of stories written between 1898 and 1909, he is insecure and the chief effect of the story is to undermine the values and assumptions with which he is satisfied at the beginning.

§

It is easy to see, therefore, why in most of the stories of this period Conrad insists on the dream-like or nightmare quality of his characters' experience. The security of their beliefs and attitudes gone, Conrad's characters find themselves in a world which offers them nothing but a 'choice of nightmares'. They may be said to have lost their bearings, for the nautical metaphor expresses their state better than any other. The phrase which Decoud writes to his sister in *Nostromo* sums up the feeling of much of this work: 'all this is life, must be life, since it is so much like a dream'.[73]

There seems, moreover, to be another reason why Conrad is so insistent on this way of expressing his characters' states of mind. He was obviously impressed by Calderon's play *La Vida es Sueño*; he mentions it in the Preface to *The Shorter Tales of Joseph Conrad* under its English title, quotes the title in his essay on Stephen Crane, and in a letter of 21 November, 1922, to Christopher Sandeman he writes: 'I felt more than ever how "*la vida es sueño*".' This work, with its insistence that the dream must be lived through to the end is surely at the back of his mind in the well-known speech of Stein in *Lord Jim*:

> A man that is born falls into a dream like a man who falls into the sea. If he tries to climb out into the air as inexperienced people endeavour to do, he drowns— . . . In the destructive element immerse . . . That was the way. To follow the dream, and again to follow the dream—and so—*ewig—usque ad finem* . . .[74]

What is so striking in Conrad's treatment of the nightmare world of these works is his emphasis that there is no escape from it. The bearings once lost cannot be found again; from the first moment of uncertainty his characters move to greater bewilderment and to a progressively clearer realization that they must experience this dream-world as fully as possible. It is, in the words of the narrator of 'Falk', 'true just as much as you are able to make it; and exactly in the way you like to make it'. And, combined with this, there tends to be an amiable contempt for those who are still relying on the simple virtues, who are not caught up in the dream—for people like Hermann in 'Falk', whose incomprehension is a mark of essential stupidity. The words of Marlow in 'Heart of Darkness' express the duty laid upon him by his experiences—the duty of following the command given in *Lord Jim* by Stein: 'I remained to dream the nightmare out to the end'.

CHAPTER V

Nostromo

IN a letter to Edward Garnett on 3 September, 1904, Conrad wrote: '*Nostromo* is finished; a fact upon which my friends may congratulate me as upon a recovery from a dangerous illness'. He began it a little before May, 1903, and finished it in September, 1904, and he seems to have suffered more agonies in the writing of it than in that of any other novel. Yet a true comment would seem to be that he worked amazingly fast; for this is one of the most complex and closely-constructed novels in the language. There are few books which, beside it, do not look—in the idiom of Henry James—as though they were not 'written'. Throughout it, we find echoes, references back and forward to incidents past or to come; and these references compel judgments or invite comparisons.

The works which we have so far considered have been remarkable for the depth of their probing into the complexities of human nature and for the intensity that they derive from Conrad's particular method of isolation which sharpens our awareness of moral issues by seeing them embodied in the fate of characters who are central to the isolated 'worlds' in which they act. But it might be felt that they obtain this depth and this force by a certain restriction of scope. Lord Jim and Captain Whalley and Marlow are not, admittedly, special cases in the sense of being obviously untypical of general human nature, and a criticism of the whole cast of thought of a commercial and colonizing society is, for instance, implied in 'Heart of Darkness'. But we may still feel that this intensive method may involve a certain narrowness of range within each book.

Whatever criticisms may be levelled against *Nostromo*,

however, it is hardly likely that it will be accused of
narrowness. It is not merely that Conrad has chosen as his
personages South American politicians of every kind, revolutionaries, a Garibaldino, an Italian seaman, a Parisian
flâneur-journalist, an Englishman and his wife, and so forth.
Width of scope is not a matter of variety of characters. What
concerns us more is the understanding which he displays of
the various forces which act in the modern world. I say 'the
modern world' advisedly, though the work was finished in
1904. The English chairman of the railway company has
not dated, and the years only show more clearly Conrad's
understanding of the American financier Holroyd, whose
'parentage was German and Scotch and English, with
remote strains of Danish and French blood, giving him the
temperament of a Puritan and an insatiable imagination of
conquest',[75] and who says:

> We in this country know just about enough to keep indoors when
> it rains. We can sit and watch. Of course, some day we shall step in.
> We are bound to. But there's no hurry. Time itself has got to wait
> on the greatest country in the whole of God's Universe. We shall be
> giving the word for everything: industry, trade, law, journalism, art,
> politics, and religion, from Cape Horn clear over to Smith's Sound,
> and beyond, too, if anything worth taking hold of turns up at the
> North Pole, And then we shall have the leisure to take in hand the
> outlying islands and continents of the earth. We shall run the world's
> business whether the world likes it or not. The world can't help it—
> and neither can we, I guess.[76]

Yet Conrad's method is the same here as in 'Heart of
Darkness' and *Lord Jim*—the method of isolation and concentration. I have already shown* the way in which the
isolation of the Occidental Province and the dominant
position of Gould are established, and all these great forces
are set in motion by the situation in Costaguana—and this
normally means, in the last analysis, by the situation in
Gould's mind. All the powers of international finance, of
idealistic love for national liberty, of European journalism,

* *v. sup.*, pp. 9 and 10, p. 12.

of commercial colonization, of the international hopes of the *risorgimento* are evoked in the book, but they appear as warring principles in Costaguana. They are present in full force, but subordinated to the complex of motives and emotions which centre on the silver of the San Tomé mine. They do not turn our attention outwards but inwards to this central theme.

Nostromo is, in every sense of the word, the biggest thing that Conrad ever did. It stands as a proof that what I have called the 'intensive' novel—the novel which has the power to be tragic—need not be even superficially narrow, need not be confined to the concerns of a small number of figures on the moors around Wuthering Heights or in Captain Ahab's ship or in the jungle village which relied on Lord Jim, that the range of its implications is no more bounded than that of a panoramic work.

Conrad's first task in this investigation of ideals, conducted on a grand scale in terms of politics and civil war as well as of individual relationships, is to convince us of the geographical and historical reality of his fictitious state. The task is elementary but nevertheless essential; we must not be allowed to feel that his creation is arbitrary, that Costaguana is an invention carefully arranged to underline his points. There can be not the slightest doubt that in this he succeeds and his method is worthy of some note because it also serves a deeper purpose in the scrutiny of the values of his characters.

He works backwards and forwards over the first part of the story, introducing his characters in relation to Sulaco, moving from one to another by their interlinking relationships, and he achieves the effect of authenticity most strikingly by his frequent changes of tone.

He opens with a note of urbane impersonality, and with a parenthesis in the first sentence as of a man conversing on something on which he knows a great deal, goes on with bland—and at this point probably unrecognized—irony to speak of the sterile promontory of Azuera ('the poor, associating by an obscure instinct of consolation the ideas of evil and wealth, will tell you that it is deadly because of its forbidden treasures'), then narrows his view to Captain Mitchell and hints at his character with the phrase: 'he accounted as most unfavourable to the orderly working of his Company the frequent changes of government brought about by revolutions of the military type'.

The effect of these changes of tone—and not less of the parenthetical insertions ('the Placido—as the saying is—goes to sleep under its black poncho')—is of a man describing something with which he is very familiar, with which he has many associations which rouse different feelings.

Every fact given in the first ten pages or so is to play a vital part in the book—the windlessness of the Golfo Placido, the Isabels, the Cordillera, the jetty; even the seemingly casual is part of the plan:

> The state possesses several harbours on its long seaboard, but except Cayta, an important place, all are either small and inconvenient inlets in an iron-bound coast—like Esmeralda, for instance, sixty miles to the south—or else mere open roadsteads exposed to the winds and fretted by the surf. [77]

But Conrad's tones are so convincingly those of a man referring to well-known places that we do not recognize this as 'setting the scene', but are rather convinced that he is choosing details from a greater body of information.

This, however, is elementary—merely a necessary *tour de force*. But the frequent changes of tone continue throughout the book with a more important function; they are one manifestation of Conrad's effort to keep us restlessly alert to every implication of his story. The sentence which describes Nostromo immediately after he has been shot is a good example of this use:

> And the voice of the resourceful Capataz de Cargadores, master and slave of the San Tomé treasure, who had been caught unawares by old Giorgio while stealing across the open towards the ravine to

E

get some more silver, answered careless and cool, but sounding
startlingly weak from the ground. [78]

The balanced and alliterated adjectives which elsewhere
seem so often to lead Conrad by their sound rather than by
their precision of sense are here under control, balanced by
the change of tone in the last phrase and in 'to get some
more silver'. Thus there is no sentimentalizing even of
Nostromo, with whose 'heroic' character Conrad himself
expressed some dissatisfaction in a letter to R. B. Cunninghame Graham, of 31 October, 1904, where he says:

> I don't defend Nostromo himself . . . truly N. is nothing at all—
> a fiction, embodied vanity of the sailor kind—a romantic mouthpiece
> of the 'people' which (I mean 'the people') frequently experience the
> very feelings to which he gives utterance. I do not defend him as a
> creation.

Nostromo is indeed conceived as a flamboyant and heroic
character, but there is nearly always a hint of the deflating
at the end of the most luxuriant passages which prevents
them from cloying. The most 'operatic' scene of the whole
book is probably the encounter of the Capataz with
Paquita on the day of the President's official visit; but it is
followed at once by Captain Mitchell's reflection that the
next time Ribiera came across the mountains it was to be
saved by Nostromo, and from this he moves naturally to the
further history of 'that fellow of mine':

> It was a fatality. A misfortune, pure and simple, sir. And that poor
> fellow of mine was right in it—right in the middle of it! A fatality,
> if ever there was one—and to my mind he has never been the same
> man since. [79]

Similarly, after the dignified description of his coming
to the treasure and finding that Decoud has taken the four
ingots to weigh down his body:

> The blank stillness of awe was succeeded by a gust of immense
> pride. There was no one in the world but Gian' Battista Fidanza,
> Capataz de Cargadores, the incorruptible and faithful Nostromo, to
> pay such a price. [80]

the deflating note is struck:

> The sun lit up the sky behind the peaks of the Cordillera. The Capataz looked down for a time upon the fall of loose earth, stones, and smashed bushes, concealing the hiding place of the silver.
> 'I must grow rich very slowly', he meditated aloud.[81]

This use of changes in tone to force the reader to a constant alertness, to a constant revaluing of the standards of his characters is only one part of the technique which Conrad uses throughout to keep us alive to his complex intention.

There is no commentator in *Nostromo* and little direct comment from Conrad himself. His method of forcing us to make judgments is normally that of juxtaposition, of allowing one section of the book to reflect implicitly on another. The part played by irony is thus very great. That *The Secret Agent* is a consistently ironic book is obvious; it is equally true, though less obvious, of *Nostromo*.

A detailed consideration of part of the chapter in which Mrs Gould sees off the troops under Barrios[82] should sufficiently demonstrate Conrad's method of not allowing us to rest for long in a stable and comfortable attitude.

The 'Tiger-killer', slightly drunk, encourages Mrs Gould, telling her that he will deal with Montero and restore order to the country; but through his speech slips the attitude of the natives:

> Señores, have no apprehension. Go on quietly making your Ferro Carril—your railways, your telegraphs. Your—There's enough wealth in Costaguana to pay for everything—or else you would not be here . . . Fear nothing, develop the country, work, work!

He interprets the gospel of Don José Avellanos:

> That is what Don José says we must do. Be enterprising! Work! Grow rich! To put Montero in a cage is my work! and when that insignificant piece of business is done, then, as Don José wishes us, we shall grow rich, one and all, like so many Englishmen, because it is money that saves a country. . . .

and then we see Don José himself, apparently not ironically for a moment:

> The terrible strain of fear and hope was telling on him, and he seemed to husband the last sparks of his fire for those oratorical efforts of which even the distant Europe was to hear.

We remember, then, that it is through Martin Decoud's journalism that the words will be preserved and this alone is enough to give them something of an effect of charlatanism.

Yet we have not been able to forget that all this takes place in the shadow of danger from Montero, and now Mrs Gould reflects that, even amongst her allies, she finds it difficult to make contact with these men of an alien race and culture; but the very way in which she phrases her reflection to herself tells us also of her isolation from her husband:

> Mrs Gould heroically concealed her dismay at the appearance of men and events so remote from her racial conventions, dismay too deep to be uttered in words even to her husband. . . . She had gone to his school of uncompromising silence.

They drive away, and a typical phrase describes the scene:

> the sparse row of telegraph poles strode obliquely clear of the town, bearing a single, almost invisible wire far into the great campo— like a slender, vibrating feeler of that progress waiting outside for a moment of peace to enter and twine itself about the weary heart of the land.

Like all Conrad's symbols, there is nothing factitious about the telegraph wire; it is a physical part of the equipment of the 'material interests' which are ultimately responsible for the departure of Barrios to fight Montero.

The party stops at the Albergo d'Italia Una to speak to the old Garibaldino, Giorgio Viola, and he talks of the equip-

ment of the troops, remembering the days when he had
fought against tyranny with home-made weapons:

> 'And yet we used to prevail against the oppressor', he concluded
> proudly.
> His animation fell; the slight gesture of his hand expressed dis-
> couragement.

We are not told directly why he is discouraged, but we can
deduce it when, in answer to his comment that the rifles
of the troops are good, Don José says:

> Yes, yes . . . We are safe. The good Señor Viola is a man of
> experience. Extremely deadly—is it not so?

The 'we' who are safe are not the 'people' of whom Viola
speaks, and he breaks out: 'And meantime they fight for
you. Blind. Esclavos' !

It is with the appearance of young Scarfe ('He was a nice
boy and Mrs Gould welcomed him') that we see most
clearly Conrad's use of juxtaposition, in a device which he
often uses—the expression in the crudest terms of what
other personages have veiled in more idealistic ones. Martin
Decoud has just pronounced Don José the only 'genuine old
Roman—*vir Romanus*—eloquent and inflexible'. Scarfe
expresses his own intransigeance:

> In a loud and youthful tone he hoped that this Montero was going
> to be licked once for all and done with. There was no saying what
> would happen to the railway if the revolution got the upper hand.
> Perhaps it would have to be abandoned. It would not be the first
> railway gone to pot in Costaguana . . . it had been such an immense
> piece of luck for him at his age to get appointed on the staff 'of a big
> thing like that—don't you know'. It would give him the pull over a
> lot of chaps all through life, he asserted. 'Therefore—down with
> Montero, Mrs Gould'.

Decoud, after they have left Scarfe, underlines the situation:

> . . . in a loud voice he began to congratulate Don José upon all the
> engineers being convinced Ribierists. The interests of all those
> foreigners was gratifying. 'You have heard this one. He is an

enlightened well-wisher. It is pleasant to think that the prosperity of Costaguana is of some use to the world'.

'He is very young', Mrs Gould remarked quietly.

'And so very wise for his age', retorted Decoud.

The chapter ends with the railway cars rumbling by:

> . . . when the ear-splitting screech of the steam-whistle for the brakes had stopped, a series of hard, battering shocks, mingled with the clanking of chain-couplings, made a tumult of blows and shaken fetters under the vault of the gate.

There is clearly no need of direct comment in passages such as this. Almost every paragraph causes us to modify our judgment and reconsider our assumptions. In no more than eight pages all the main issues of the book are touched upon and the full weight of criticism of the 'material interests' which oppose Montero and of the habits of mind which they cause is subtly asserted.

The railway trucks which make the sound of shaken fetters, like the telegraph wire, are both concrete facts, playing their part in the plot, and symbols of the enslavement of the country. Throughout the book, the moral, the psychological and the spiritual issues are embodied naturally in outward objects. The most potent of these symbols is the silver, which Conrad once described as the real hero of the book.* Ironically described as 'incorruptible metal', it is most powerfully used in the scenes in the lighter where it is both heavy material and a principle of corruption, and in the small boat where it serves to sink the body of Decoud so

---

* In a letter to Ernst Bendz of 7 March, 1923, in which he thanks him for a pamphlet in English published in Göteborg: 'I will take the liberty to point out that Nostromo has never been intended for the hero of the *Tale of the Seaboard*. Silver is the pivot of the moral and material events, affecting the lives of everybody in the tale. That this was my deliberate purpose there can be no doubt. I struck the first note of my intention in the unusual form which I gave to the title of the First Part, by calling it "The Silver of the Mine", and by telling the story of the enchanted treasure on Azuera, which, strictly speaking, has nothing to do with the rest of the novel. The word 'silver' occurs almost at the very beginning of the story proper, and I took care to introduce it in the very last paragraph, which would, perhaps, have been better without the phrase which contains that key-word.'

that no trace of him ever appears, leaving Nostromo with the treasure which has four ingots missing.*

Its function is summed up in this description of Mrs Gould:

> . . . she had laid her unmercenary hands, with an eagerness that made them tremble, upon the first silver ingot turned out still warm from the mould; and by her imaginative estimate of its power she endowed that lump of metal with a justificative conception, as though it were not a mere fact, but something far-reaching and impalpable, like the true expression of an emotion or the emergence of a principle. [83]

Many of these themes and symbols recur again and again throughout the book, and often the implied comparisons are more than single. This becomes clear if we follow the one which occurs first—the treasure hidden on Azuera. It is first mentioned in the opening chapter as part of the description of the scenery of the Golfo Placido and the province of Sulaco:

> The poor, associating by an obscure instinct of consolation the ideas of evil and wealth, will tell you that it [Azuera] is deadly because of its forbidden treasures . . . the two gringos, spectral and alive, are believed to be dwelling to this day among the rocks, under the fatal spell of their success. Their souls cannot tear themselves away from their bodies mounting guard over the discovered treasure. They are now rich and hungry and thirsty. . . . [84]

That this is echoed again and again with reference to Nostromo and his enslavement by the treasure, is obvious enough. 'It is as if I were taking a curse upon me',[85] he says, as he sails out in the lighter, and when he comes to the buried treasure after Decoud's death 'the silver of San Tomé was provided now with a faithful and lifelong slave'.[86] He is aware of this himself; when he returns from one of

---

* Here Conrad draws—typically for him—on the event described in *The Mirror of the Sea* (1906) when Dominic Cervoni's nephew, Cesar, trying to betray them and steal the gold which the boat carried, was knocked overboard and sunk by the weight of his loot.

his voyages to find the lighthouse being built over his hoard

> he compared himself to the legendary Gringos, neither dead nor alive, bound down to their conquest of unlawful wealth on Azuera. [87]

The silver finally kills him, because he has to accept Linda as his betrothed for fear of being forbidden the island and, meeting Giselle secretly, he is shot by mistake.

But the implications are extended to Charles Gould. Towards the end of the book, word is brought to Mrs Gould that 'The master remains to sleep at the mountain to-night', and she reflects that her husband is

> incorrigible in his hard, determined service of the material interests to which he had pinned his faith in the triumph of order and justice. Poor boy! [88]

Shortly after, she has to console Giselle for the death of her lover. The parallel between the cases of Nostromo and of her husband is explicit:

> 'Console yourself, child. Very soon he would have forgotten you for his treasure'.
> 'Señora, he loved me. He loved me', Giselle whispered despairingly. 'He loved me as no-one had ever been loved before'.
> 'I have been loved, too', Mrs Gould said in a severe tone. [89]

It is indeed true that 'The mine had got hold of Charles Gould with a grip as deadly as ever it had laid upon his father' [90] and Nostromo's remark to Monygham, when he is ostensibly speaking of Sotillo, applies not only to his own case but also to that of 'The King of Sulaco':

> There is no getting away from a treasure that once fastens upon your mind. [91]

But the obsessions of Nostromo and of Gould are not of the same kind. Nostromo is moved partly by greed, partly by his feeling that he cannot give back the treasure with the four ingots missing, and most by a superstitious belief that the treasure is accursed and that he is the man who must bear the curse, for 'It was paid for by a soul lost and by a vanished life'. In this he has been encouraged by Monygham, who tells him, when they discuss the reward he should have for the dangerous task of getting the silver out of Sulaco:

'Illustrious Capataz, for taking the curse of death upon my back, as you call it, nothing else but the whole treasure would do.'[92]

The chains which bind Charles Gould to his silver mine are chains of idealism: partly a desire to succeed in an enterprise which has killed his father, partly the hope of a 'liberal' future for Costaguana. Conrad is not concerned with anything so simple as a mere study of greed, of a man estranged from his wife by gross material desires for wealth. Nor—though he is well aware of the power of 'material interests', of international finance and commerce—is it merely the conflict between them and personal integrity which concerns him. The origin of Gould's devotion to the mine is idealistic and the mixture of emotions which remains to the end is well shown in such a subtle comment as:

The mine had corrupted his judgment by making him sick of bribing and intriguing merely to have his work left alone from day to day.[93]

The mine is, for those who work at it, 'the fountain of honour, of prosperity, and peace'. For the Indians it has 'a protecting and invincible virtue as though it were a fetish made by their own hands'.[94]*

Gould's motive in first deciding to go out to Costaguana to work the mine is 'a vague idea of rehabilitation'; he feels that by succeeding he can rehabilitate the memory of his father. We are told, when he hears of the death of his father:

Action is consolatory. It is the enemy of thought and the friend of flattering illusions. Only in the conduct of our action can we find

---

* There is an echo here of Mrs Gould's reflection: 'It had been an idea. She had watched it with misgivings turning into a fetish, and now the fetish had grown into a monstrous and crushing weight' (p. 221).

the sense of mastery over the Fates. For his action the mine was obviously the only field . . . The mine had been the cause of an absurd moral disaster; its working must be made a serious and moral success. He owed it to the dead man's memory.[95]

The idea of social progress is in his mind from the start. Speaking of his uncle, he says:

. . . he was no politician. He simply stood up for social order out of pure love for rational liberty and from his hatred of oppression. There was no nonsense about him. He went to work in his own way because it seemed right, just as I feel I must lay hold of that mine.[96]

Hence he seeks the help of the financier Holroyd, with his 'purer forms of Christianity', and involves himself in the politics of Costaguana. He needs peace and order for the development of the mine; the responsible elements in Costaguana—the 'Blancos'—need the support of the silver of the mine to succeed in bringing about a better state in their country.

Gould's idealism is stressed again and again, even by those, such as Martin Decoud, who are unsympathetic to him. But Decoud does him less than justice when he says to Mrs Gould:

Are you aware to what point he has idealized the existence, the worth, the meaning of the San Tomé mine? . . . he cannot act or exist without idealizing every simple feeling, desire, or achievement. He could not believe his own motives if he did not make them first a part of some fairy tale. The earth is not quite good enough from him, I fear.[97]

Decoud does not know that his devotion to the mine— a devotion so great that it continually keeps him from his wife—springs originally from idealism.

The idealistic obsession follows its inevitable course; there is no turning back in the service of the mine and, while we realize the truth of the words of Hernandez's emissary: 'Your own officials do not oppress the people in the gorge . . . You are a just man and a powerful one', we see that it leads to 'that sentimental unfaithfulness which surrenders her [Mrs Gould's] happiness, her life, to the seduction of an idea'. And we know that Mrs Gould cannot hope to succeed in her mission to save him from the effects of what Decoud correctly sees as 'that cold and over-mastering passion, which she dreads more than if it were an infatuation for another woman'.[98]

Mrs Gould's own awareness of what has happened to the relationship between them is rendered in one very fine and subtle passage; the news of Decoud's death has just reached them and Charles Gould is considering what he can do now that the silver is lost:

> Mrs Gould watched his abstraction with dread. It was a domestic and frightful phenomenon that darkened and chilled the house for her like a thunder-cloud passing over the sun. Charles Gould's fits of abstraction depicted the energetic concentration of a will haunted by a fixed idea. A man haunted by a fixed idea is insane. He is dangerous even if that idea is an idea of justice; for may he not bring the heaven down pitilessly upon a loved head? The eyes of Mrs Gould, watching her husband's profile, filled with tears again. And again she seemed to see the despair of the unfortunate Antonia. 'What would I have done if Charley had been drowned while we were engaged'? she exclaimed, mentally, with horror.[99]

Antonia's love for Decoud links itself in her mind with her own love for her husband, but thoughts of her own un-happiness are what remind her of Decoud's death. Antonia's despair will have something in common with her own, for her hopes of happiness have been just as effectively destroyed as those of the girl will be, and to find a time of happiness in her memories she has to go back to the period of her engagement. She cries out: 'Antonia will kill herself!' but 'This cry fell into the silence of the room with strangely little effect', for Charles Gould's mind is still taken up with his plans about what he shall write to Holroyd. He has no time to spare for thinking of Antonia, nor, by implication, of his own relationship with his wife.

But with the development of the political situation and Gould's closer view of the political 'idealists' with whom he has linked himself comes disillusionment for him. When he sees the deputation from the Provincial Assembly waiting to call on Montero, we are told that:

> The feeling of compassion for these men, struck with a strange impotence in the toils of moral degradation, did not induce him to make a sign. He suffered from his fellowship in evil with them too much,[100]

and he says to Monygham:

> The words one knows so well have a nightmarish meaning in this country. Liberty, democracy, patriotism, government—all of them have a flavour of folly and murder.[101]

But disillusion does not deliver him from his bondage to the mine; he remains the servant of those 'material interests' which he has invoked to assist him in his desire for 'a serious and moral success'. We see his fetish at the end, in Nostromo's words, as

> hateful and immense, lording it by its vast wealth over the valour, the toil, the fidelity of the poor, over war and peace, over the labours of the town, the sea, and the Campo.[102]

If we are inclined to discredit Nostromo as seeking some justification for his theft, we have also Dr Monygham's measured words to Mrs Gould:

> There is no peace, and no rest in the development of material interests. They have their law, and their justice. But it is founded on expediency, and is inhuman . . . Mrs Gould, the time approaches when all that the Gould Concession stands for shall weigh as heavily upon the people as the barbarism, cruelty, and misrule of a few years back.[103]

The final result of the early ideal, which has been the inspiration of Mrs Gould as well as of her husband, is summed up, with an ironic echo of *The Times* correspondent's phrase:

> With a prophetic vision she saw herself surviving alone the degradation of her young ideal of life, of love, of work—all alone in the Treasure House of the World.[104]

But it is important to realize that Mrs Gould is not merely a victim; she is not, like some of Conrad's later heroines, flawless and adorned with a blaze of rhetoric. Her idealism has walked side by side with that of her husband, encouraging him in his course. When Charles Gould begins to feel the spell of the mine, just after the death of his father, with

> another form of enchantment, more suitable to his youth, into whose magic formula there entered hope, vigour and self-confidence, instead of weary indignation and despair[105]

then:

> . . . at once her delight in him, lingering with half-open wings like those birds that cannot rise easily from a flat level, found a pinnacle from which to soar up into the skies.[106]

Though she saves the Viola's house from the devastating march of progress, and though it is her water-colour sketch which preserves the memory of the mountain water-fall before its ravine was 'only a big trench half filled up with the refuse of excavations and tailings', yet she, too, has been subtly corrupted by the mine.

When Decoud brings her the news of Montero's victory he persuades her to conceal the news from her husband, reminding her that her care for the physical well-being of the workpeople depends on the silver. She takes part in the game of 'material interests' and at the end of the book she reproaches herself:

> . . . she did not say she hated the mere mention of that silver. Frankness personified, she remembered with an exaggerated horror that for the first and last time of her life she had concealed the truth from her husband about that very silver. She had been corrupted by her fears at that time, and she had never forgiven herself . . . the silver . . . would never have come down if her husband had been made acquainted with the news brought by Decoud.[107]

None can escape responsibility for the devotion to the silver—whether it is seen as an instrument of political or social or personal power—which kills Decoud and corrupts the apparently incorruptible Nostromo. The silver of the mine is indeed, as Conrad said, the real hero of the book, for although the Goulds and Nostromo are, in their different ways, the central characters—those on whom the fates of the others depend—yet the novel is a study of interlocking relationships and values centring round the treasure. And, with the exception of the austere and beautiful Antonia, who remains rather misty to the end* and Giorgio Viola, who dies 'rugged, undecayed, like an old oak uprooted by a treacherous gust of wind', all those others into whose hearts and minds we see are observed with the same penetrating and usually ironic scrutiny. And it is always the silver, either as wealth or as a double-edged weapon of political or personal idealism, which searches out their weaknesses. But the unity of the book does not depend on a restriction of the problems raised to those of the two central figures nor on a repetition of the same problems in the minor characters.

It must be emphasized, too, that the reactions of the characters to one another are of great significance. There is no mere use of one character to comment on another; the comment also tells us more about the commentator. In this book there are no author's mouthpieces. It is, for example, precisely in the inadequacy of his comment on Gould that we see what is wrong with Martin Decoud.

His perceptions are clear, up to a point. He can make Mrs Gould see more clearly her husband's idealization of his mine, he can make her give in, unable to resist his analysis. But he is not, as I have pointed out,† quite correct, and there is in his argument too much of the pleasure of pointing out weaknesses and a too ready generalization— the superficiality of the man who works with people and

* *v. inf.*, p. 63 footnote
† *v. sup.*, p. 58

ideas as counters in a game. He emphasizes continually that he is a 'realist' in such passages as:

> What is a conviction? A particular view of our personal advantage either practical or emotional. No one is a patriot for nothing. The word serves us well. But I am clear-sighted, and I shall not use that word to you, Antonia![108]

or:

> I cannot endow my personal desires with a shining robe of silk and jewels. Life is not for me a moral romance derived from the tradition of a pretty fairy tale. No, Mrs Gould; I am practical. I am not afraid of my motives.[109]

There is nothing behind these facile phrases but a desire for Antonia and a delight in being disabused, and they do not survive as-sufficient motive for living when he is alone on the island.

This seems the time to say something which probably needs to be said, but which has little place in a discussion of *Nostromo* as a novel as distinct from that of the interest which it possesses as a revelation of Conrad's own life: the fact that, in his description of Costaguana, he seems at times to be thinking of the Poland of his boyhood. For it is Decoud who is the mouthpiece of most of these remarks, of such judgments as: ' "We are a wonderful people, but it has always been our fate to be"—he did not say "robbed", but added, after a pause—"exploited". ' Antonia Avellanos, he tells us in the 'Author's Note' to the Collected Edition, is modelled on his 'first love,'* and he tells how this Polish girl used to attack his levities—'very much like poor Decoud'. We may look at the figures of Martin Decoud and Joseph Conrad and see no resemblance between the fictitious creation and his creator, but it seems probable that Conrad himself saw some link. Decoud is a 'hollow man' like Kurtz in 'Heart of Darkness'; and with Kurtz,

---

* The somewhat uncritical treatment of her is in keeping with this. It is the nearest thing in this book to the romantic and idealizing view of his heroines which we find in his later novels.

into whose emptiness could flow whatever of evil surrounded him, Marlow had felt an 'unforeseen partnership'. It is
not, I think, fanciful to believe that Conrad felt such a
partnership with Decoud.

Nevertheless, as I have said, I do not think that the
knowledge that he had Poland and, perhaps, some early
feelings of his own in mind can help us very much in a
criticism of the novel as a novel. It does not seem to have
led to any important lack of detachment, to any appre-
ciable flaws, to any confusion in the judgments which he
makes. It may have been partly responsible for the agonies
which he described himself as undergoing in the composition of it, but it does not thrust itself upon us as a distraction.

Even Dr Monygham, upon whose judgment of the mine
we seem intended to rely most, is seen with the same eyes as
the others. He is not a victim of greed, nor of misplaced
political idealism, nor does he elevate material objects into
sentimental principles. His comment on himself could have
come from Decoud's lips:

> I put no spiritual value into my desires, or my opinions, or my
> actions. They have not enough vastness to give me room for self-
> flattery.[110]

Like Decoud, too, he is moved only by a love for one
person—in his case for Mrs Gould—and this love makes
him ruthless to everybody else. By deceiving Sotillo about
the position of the silver he sees a chance of helping her, and
so he is not moved when Nostromo says:

> Perhaps, if you had not confirmed Sotillo in his madness, he would
> have been in no haste to give the estrapade to that miserable Hirsch.[111]

The judgment on his devotion—and on its fanaticism—
follows:

> The doctor started at the suggestion. But his devotion, absorbing
> all sensibilities, had left his heart steeled against remorse and pity.[112]

There is some justice in Nostromo's view that he is 'a
dangerous man'. The view of the Capataz at the end is that

Monygham is 'the worst despiser of all the poor—of the people', and the doctor responds with 'temperamental enmity to Nostromo' and contrasts himself with 'the man who had lived his own life on the assumption of unbroken fidelity, rectitude, and courage'.[113] His devotion to Mrs Gould becomes an obsession, making his heart 'implacable in the expansion of its tenderness'[114] causing him 'to dislike everybody who approached Mrs Gould with any intimacy'. We finally see his situation presented in an image which links his devotion and the guilt which he bears for having been prepared to sacrifice others for it with the central theme of the book:

> Dr Monygham had grown older, with his head steel-grey and the unchanged expression of his face, living on the inexhaustible treasure of his devotion drawn upon in the secret of his heart like a store of unlawful wealth.[115]

The changes in tone and the juxtaposition of different themes and points of view is paralleled on a larger scale by the structure of the book, which throws into relief the central theme as distinct from the plot. The arrangement of different sections, the frequent shifts in time and in viewpoint are often designed to sharpen our apprehension of the issues involved, to force us to make comparisons and to see links between incidents and emotions which are not necessarily related by the causal logic of plot.

Some of the shifts seem to have a practical motive alone behind them. Conrad has set himself the task of telling the stories of so many people that it is essential from time to time to break the flow of narration. Such a shift is the regression, after the description of the riot near the Albergo d'Italia Una (in Part I, Chapters II and IV) to the life of the Violas in Sulaco. The move is made with ease and with no sense of strain by using the picture of Garibaldi, lit up as soon as Viola opens the door after the departure of the rioters, as its vehicle.

A consideration of how Conrad manages the introduction

F

of his characters and tells us everything that we need to know about their previous histories and their interrelations fills one with admiration for his skill; one after another his personages are presented, linked with ones whom we have already got to know (Mrs Gould, for instance, is first mentioned towards the end of the passage just considered as having given his spectacles to Viola); then, later, the narration returns to them, enlarges on them, shows more of their relations with other people, and thus, gradually, the whole picture of Sulaco is built up.

But, fascinating though a study of this might be, it need not detain us. Conrad's ability to control the mechanics of the story without wearying us is obvious, and though this manipulation may fill other writers with admiration or envious despair it will not help us to see more clearly the significance of the novel.

There are, however, these other shifts which are significant in that, by contrast and unexpected combination or by the deliberate disappointment of expectations, they force us to think more clearly about the meaning of his story.

A notable and significant breach of the time-sequence occurs in Part I. The general movement of this part is:

Pages 1–33. The day of Ribiera's escape and the defeat of the rioters by Nostromo and his Cargadores.

Pages 34–43. Eighteen months earlier; the arrival of the chairman of the railway board, the dinner party and the high hopes of prosperity from Ribiera's appointment.

Pages 44–116. The early history of the San Tomé mine, the death of Charles Gould's father, his own decision to make the mine a 'moral success', his marriage, his bargain with Holroyd, his disgust with the unscrupulous politics of Sulaco, and the life of the Goulds in the town.

Pages 116–131. A return to the day of the dinner party.

As a result of this movement to and fro we see the financial string-pulling which is at the back of the politics which the hidalgos pursue with such fine speeches, and, more important, we realize throughout the story of the youthful idealism

of the Goulds that it is leading to the remark of the railway
chairman, occurring in the earlier section:

> We can't give you your ecclesiastical court back again; but you
> shall have more steamers, a railway, a telegraph-cable—a future in
> the great world which is worth infinitely more than any amount of
> ecclesiastical past. You shall be brought in touch with something
> greater than two viceroyalties.[116]*

The time-sequence is broken, the viewpoint changed, in
short, so as to bring out more clearly the pattern of values
which underlies the story. Conrad is aiming at no effect of
surprise; the final results are given before the events which
lead up to them. There is no suggestion of the 'irony of
fate' in the results of Charles Gould's idealism. The triumph
of the values of Holroyd and of the chairman of the railway
company '(from London)' and his own corruption are
inherent in it from the start.

The most striking of these shifts, however, occurs in the
first half of Part III, Chapter X. During the preceding
chapters we have been in the midst of the fighting; the
first nine chapters of Part III flow forward chronologically,
save for parenthetical passages on the lives of Dr Monygham
and the Monteros and on Hirsch's death and for a few pages
at the beginning of Chapter II which fulfil much the same
function as the chapter which we are here considering.
But in Chapter X the sequence is broken; we are transported
many years ahead and we listen to 'Fussy Joe' Mitchell's
reminiscences. The fighting is a distant event at the beginning of the period in which Mitchell is 'allowed to attain
the term of his usefulness in ease and dignity at the head of
the enormously extended service.[117] Any tension, any
expectation of a grand climax with Don Pépé marching on
the town at the head of the mine-workers and Barrios'
forces arriving by sea from Cayta, is frustrated. The fate

---

* Both the railway and the telegraph cable, it will be remembered, play their
part in Part II, Chapter IV, *v. sup.*, pp. 52 and 54.

of Sulaco and its inhabitants is told us casually as part of an elderly man's boring gossip:

> Standing under that very gateway, sir, with some young engineer-fellows, ready to defend that house where we had received so much kindness and hospitality, I saw the first and last charge of Pedrito's horsemen . . . The Intendencia, now President's Palace . . . Pedrito Montero had Don Carlos led out to be shot . . . This is the famous Hernandez, Minister of War . . . He was preparing to hang Dr Monygham. . . .

and so it continues until 'the coxswain's voice at the door, announcing that the gig was ready, closed the cycle'.

Anyone so unperceptive as to read *Nostromo* as a story of adventure will exclaim in horror at this throwing away of a series of magnificent climaxes. But one would need to be very unperceptive, for here Conrad is only making more emphatic what has surely been obvious all along—that his theme is not revolution and physical action but the progress of 'material interests' and the corruption of the hearts of those who invoke them in their idealism.

The irony which is omnipresent in the novel is at its strongest in this chapter. 'Fussy Joe's' judgments throughout underline the contrast between naïve views of 'progress' and our knowledge of what this progress means for the intimate lives of Charles Gould and his wife, of Nostromo, of Decoud, of the Violas. We compare: 'Sulaco National Bank there, with the sentry boxes each side of the gate' and 'Anzani's nephews converted the business into a company' with the inscription on the tomb of Don José Avellanos: 'Died in the woods of Los Hatos worn out with his life-long struggle for Right and Justice at the dawn of the New Era'. The New Era seems, in essence, very like the old.

Every heavy platitude has ironical repercussions.* Of

---

* This is true not only of this chapter. Cf. Mitchell's comment when 'three gentlemen' come to visit the Goulds from San Francisco (p. 68): 'This marks an epoch'.

Mrs Gould he says:

> The kindest, most gracious woman the sun ever shone upon.
> A great position, sir. A great position. First lady in Sulaco—far
> before the President's wife.

of Monygham:

> He saved us all from the deadly incubus of Sotillo, when a more
> particular man might have failed.

He is an enthusiastic supporter of the material interests
which have triumphed with the triumph of political order:

> ... the 'Treasure House of the World', as *The Times* man calls
> Sulaco in his book, was saved intact for civilization—for a great
> future, sir.

and we hear that 'Don Carlos Gould was packing up his
trunks bound on a mission to San Francisco and Washington'.
It is therefore natural that 'The equestrian statue that used to
stand on the pedestal over there has been removed. It was an
anachronism'.

He ends:

> Miss Avellanos burst into tears only when he [Nostromo] told her
> how Decoud had happened to say that his plan would be a glorious
> success ... And there's no doubt, sir, that it is. It is a success.

By the naïve standards of Mitchell, judged by faith in
'progress' and good parliamentary government and the
physical safety of the law-abiding citizen, it is indeed.
But the book has shown us the disastrous nature of this
success and we know the full truth of Fussy Joe's comment
on the mine: 'A great power, this, for good and evil, sir.
A great power'.

CHAPTER VI

'The Secret Sharer'

THOUGH it was not published until 1912 in the volume 'Twixt Land and Sea, 'The Secret Sharer' was written in November, 1909. Conrad had taken up and set aside Chance, finished The Secret Agent, just completed A Personal Record, and was engaged in writing Under Western Eyes, which he finished two months later.

It is a remarkable story and its extraordinary virtues have attracted surprisingly little attention. It belongs very obviously, in the nature of the interests displayed and in some similarities of treatment, to the same phase of his writing as 'Heart of Darkness', Lord Jim and Nostromo. But it marks the end of this period. The previous works show the central character confronted by some realization of the nature of his beliefs or by some 'deadly incubus'—the knowledge of the link with Mr Kurtz or Gentleman Brown, the disturbing awareness of 'the foundation of all the emotions' or of the disastrous results of Don Carlos Gould's idealism. From this knowledge or from these relationships there is no escape; in the nature of the case no solution of the problems is possible. The narrator of 'The Secret Sharer' is similarly faced by the realization of a bond between him and Leggatt, but he finds a solution; at the end of the story he frees himself from the haunting presence of his 'other self'.

The setting of the story is typical of Conrad's work in its emphasis on the isolation of the little self-contained world of the ship and on the supremely important position of the narrator–captain. So far as outward power is concerned, he reflects: 'I could do what I liked, with no one to say nay to me within the whole circle of the horizon'.[118]

At the end, when he is giving Leggatt, the secret sharer of his cabin, an opportunity to escape, although he seems to his officers and men to be wantonly running the ship aground yet he is still obeyed. The crew know that their safety is in his hands, yet he is still the captain and they leave their fate to him.

The intruder on this isolation is Leggatt, the fugitive who swims out to the ship, and it is made abundantly clear that he is only able to come on board because of the state of mind of the captain, a state in which he feels 'somewhat of a stranger' to himself. He decides to set no anchor-watch and to stay on deck alone and explains that:

> My strangeness, which had made me sleepless, had prompted that unconventional arrangement, as if I had expected in those solitary hours of the night to get on terms with the ship of which I knew nothing, manned by men of whom I knew very little more.[119]

It seems at first as though he will achieve his purpose. In a passage whose irony very soon becomes apparent, he says:

> . . . as I passed the door of the forecastle I heard a deep, quiet, trustful sigh of some sleeper inside. And suddenly I rejoiced in the great security of the sea as compared with the unrest of the land, in my choice of that untempted life presenting no disquieting problems, invested with an elementary moral beauty by the absolute straight-forwardness of its appeal and by the singleness of its purpose.
>
> The riding-light in the fore-rigging burned with a clear, untroubled, as if symbolic flame, confident and bright in the mysterious shades of the night.[120]

Immediately after this he notices that the rope-ladder has not been hauled in as it should, but checks his annoyance with the reflection that his own action is responsible for this. The ladder is there because he has decided to dismiss all hands and keep the watch himself in the endeavour to over-come his feeling of 'strangeness'. When he tries to pull the ladder aboard, he finds the man hanging on the bottom of it. Leggatt asserts later, when he is the 'secret sharer' of the narrator's thoughts, that it was the ladder alone which saved him.

> I wasn't capable of swimming round as far as your rudder-chains [he says] And, lo and behold! there was a ladder to get hold of.[121]

The captain does not consciously decide to conceal the fugitive, any more than Marlow consciously decides to accept the 'unforeseen partnership' with Kurtz. As soon as he sees him, he reflects later: 'A mysterious communication was established already between us two—in the face of that silent, darkened tropical sea'.[122] Leggatt speaks of him as talking to him quietly—'as if you had expected me'. The closeness of this mysterious communication is emphasized from the very start of their relationship, first because of the accident of a similarity of clothes:

> In a moment [the captain says] he had concealed his damp body in a sleeping-suit of the same grey-stripe pattern as the one I was wearing and followed me like my double on the poop.[123]

As Leggatt tells his story it is as though the captain were seeing his own reflection 'in the depths of a sombre and immense mirror', so that he can say: 'I saw it all going on as though I were myself inside that other sleeping-suit'.[124] There is a phrase which is strongly reminiscent of those which tell of the link between Lord Jim and Gentleman Brown: 'He appealed to me as if our experiences had been as identical as our clothes'.[125] This is, above all, what is stressed—the bond between the captain and the intruder with his burden of guilt. The bond is the closest possible; Leggatt is described as his 'double' or his 'other self' more than twenty times in the course of the story. When the captain of the *Sephora* comes in search of Leggatt and says that he 'wasn't exactly the sort for the chief mate of a ship like the *Sephora*', the captain reflects:

> I had become so connected in thoughts and impressions with the secret sharer of my cabin that I felt as if I, personally, were being given to understand that I, too, was not the sort that would have done for the chief mate of a ship like the *Sephora*.[126]

He feels 'utterly incapable of playing the part of ignorance properly',[127] so that, as he says;

> I could not, I think, have met him by a direct lie, also for psychological (not moral) reasons. If he had only known how afraid I was of his putting my feeling of identity with the other to the test! But, strangely enough—(I thought of it only afterward)—I believe that he was not a little disconcerted by the reverse side of that weird situation, by something in me that reminded him of the man he was seeking—suggested a mysterious similitude to the young fellow he had distrusted and disliked from the first.[128]*

The link is not, as in 'Heart of Darkness' or Lord Jim, with someone obviously wicked. The crime of Leggatt is a very modified one in the eyes of the narrator and we remember that when a reviewer described him as a 'murderous ruffian' Conrad said that he was 'simply knocked over' by such a misunderstanding. But there is, in Leggatt, a feeling of guilt, the knowledge that he has, like Lord Jim, transgressed against the code of society. He can speak of the man he has killed as one of the 'miserable devils that have no business to live at all', but he is prepared to accept 'the "brand of Cain" business'. 'I was ready enough', he says, 'to go off wandering on the face of the earth'.

We are not, moreover, concerned with the precise nature of Leggatt's offence, for there is no indication that the captain feels any shadow of guilt specifically because the man he is hiding is a murderer. Leggatt is an embodiment of his original feeling of being 'a stranger' to himself, of that fear that there are parts of himself which he has not yet brought into the light of day and that these aspects of his personality may interfere with 'that ideal conception of one's own personality every man sets up for himself secretly'. What disturbs him is that there is a secret sharer at all, for he brings to light his own suspected insecurity.

The captain leads a life of whispers and sudden concealments and, inevitably, his nerves begin to go to pieces. He

---

* It should be noted that the narrator has said that physically 'He was not a bit like me, really'.

shouts at men or whispers suddenly, stops men from entering his state-room, feeling all the time that 'it would take very little to make me a suspect person in the eyes of the ship's company'.[129] They begin to assume that he is either mad or drinking, and his mental state expresses itself for him, too, in the knowledge that it impairs his ability to command.

> This [he says] is not the place to enlarge upon the sensations of a man who feels for the first time a ship move under his feet to his own independent word. In my case they were not unalloyed. I was not wholly alone with my command; for there was that stranger in my cabin. Or rather, I was not completely and wholly with her. Part of me was absent. That mental feeling of being in two places at once affected me physically as if the mood of secrecy had penetrated my very soul.[130]

As a result the orders which should spring to his lips without thinking or reflection do not come; 'all unconscious alertness' deserts him; it requires an effort of will to call his mind back from his 'secret double' to the 'conditions of the moment'.

Every detail of the story is perfectly concrete, perfectly naturalistic, yet this is far more a nightmare story than any other—far more than such obviously 'painful' stories as 'Freya of the Seven Isles', which appeared in the same volume. The feeling of 'duality' is pushed to the point at which the captain fears for his sanity, because this 'confused sensation of being in two places at once' is set against his endeavour to retain his grasp on normality—embodied here as the ability to command his ship and deal with his crew. During breakfast, on the morning after Leggatt has come aboard, he says:

> ... all the time the dual working of my mind distracted me almost to the point of insanity. I was constantly watching myself, my secret self, as dependent on my actions as my own personality, sleeping on that bed, behind that door which faced me as I sat at the head of the table. It was very much like being mad, only it was worse because one was aware of it.[131]

On the fourth day of 'miserable juggling with the unavoidable' he reaches the climax of this torment of trying to reconcile the knowledge of the secret sharer with his duty as shipmaster. The steward goes to hang up the captain's coat, opens the door of the bathroom, where Leggatt is concealed, and does not see him hiding in the bath. The captain waits for the inevitable discovery, and, when it does not come, his bewilderment and his mixture of feelings about Leggatt come out in his first reflection:

'Saved', I thought. 'But no! Lost! Gone! He was gone!'[132]

At this stage in his experience he actually fears that he may already be insane.

> ... an irresistible doubt of his bodily existence flitted through my mind [he says]. Can it be, I asked myself, that he is not visible to other eyes than mine? It was like being haunted ... I think I had come creeping quietly as near insanity as any man who has not actually gone over the border.[133]

But from this position escape is possible, as it is not possible for the central characters of the earlier stories. This is because the situation of the narrator in 'The Secret Sharer' is a stage nearer the purely symbolic than that dealt with in the other works. As I have shown, the presence of Leggatt is so nightmarish, not because he makes the captain aware of any inadequacy or wrongness in his ideas and beliefs, but rather because the relationship between them is itself an objective correlative of such knowledge. After the death of Kurtz, Marlow is left with his mind uneasy and with the feeling that the last words of the dying man were 'a moral victory', but in 'The Secret Sharer' the whole of the narrator's 'strangeness' has been so completely embodied in the person of Leggatt that seemingly it can be got rid of.

Leggatt can, in fact, be marooned on one of the islands that fringe the Gulf of Siam. But the captain feels that he cannot do this easily. Although he knows that he may be endangering his ship by taking such a risk, he feels that, as he says, 'It was now a matter of conscience to shave the

land as close as possible'.[134] Clearly it is not physical con-
siderations alone which determine this need; Leggatt can
swim too well for that. It seems, rather, that the captain
feels that to exorcise his 'other self' he must run as close to
disaster as possible, knowing all the time, as he says, that

> all my future, the only future for which I was fit, would perhaps
> go irretrievably to pieces in any mishap to my first command.[135]

Thus, finally, the narrator and Leggatt are separated; even
the hat which the captain thrusts on the fugitive's head*
falls off in the water and acts as a mark by which he can
gauge the progress of the ship.

> Now I had what I wanted [the captain says]—the saving mark for
> my eyes. But I hardly thought of my other self, now gone from the
> ship, to be hidden forever from all friendly faces . . . I watched the
> hat—the expression of my sudden pity for his mere flesh. It had
> been meant to save his homeless head from the dangers of the sun.
> And now—behold—it was saving the ship, by serving me for a mark
> to help out the ignorance of my strangeness.[136]

Now at last the captain can feel certain of his ability to
command, as he could not when he gave his first order and
knew that he was not 'wholly alone' with his command.
Now he can say:

> Already the ship was drawing ahead. And I was alone with her.
> Nothing! no one in the world should stand now between us, throw-
> ing a shadow on the way of silent knowledge and mute affection,
> the perfect communion of a seaman with his first command.[137]

'Strangeness'—the knowledge of the 'secret double'—has
been exorcised and normality restored.

§

This story, as I have pointed out, marks the end of one
phase of Conrad's work; the preoccupations are funda-

---

* The degree of identification is, perhaps, stronger here than anywhere else in
the story. 'I saw *myself* wandering barefooted, bareheaded, the sun beating on my
dark poll. I snatched off my floppy hat and tried hurriedly in the dark to ram it
on my other self' (p. 138, my italics).

mentally the same as in the earlier books but the situation is so presented that a solution can be offered. It is noticeable that after this a change comes over his writing, and when we consider the form which it takes we are struck at once by a parallel between it and 'The Secret Sharer'. The story might almost be an allegory of Conrad's future development.

The Conrad of the group of stories and novels which we have been considering is as obsessed by the consciousness of the 'other self' as the narrator of 'The Secret Sharer'. There is a potentially evil or discreditable side to the natures of all his central characters, a seed of corruption in all their idealisms, a suspicion that all our most elevated feelings derive at bottom from the same root as the hunger of Falk which had to be satisfied by cannibalism.

There can be little of quietness or optimism or security in such a view of human life, and the works are indeed disturbing and, like Marlow's reminiscences, 'inconclusive'. The price of peace of mind for Conrad seems to be much the same as it is for the narrator of this story. He turns away from these preoccupations. In the later works, as we shall see, there is no longer this emphasis on the sense of guilt and this indefinable compact with the 'secret double'. The simple virtues of honesty, courage and fidelity to one's comrades, whose insufficiency has been one of the main themes of works like 'Heart of Darkness' and *Nostromo*, are in the later books sufficient guides. It would, of course, be too much to say that no doubts of them are ever expressed, but such expressions are rarely more than perfunctory and they never carry the same weight of feeling and criticism as in the early books. One consequence of this removal of tension from the experience of his central figures is that his characters tend more and more to fall into two groups—the good and the bad.

The contrast in outlook is very clearly seen if we

compare the significance of the description in this story of the

> great security of the sea . . . that untempted life presenting no dis-
> quieting problems, invested with an elementary moral beauty by the
> absolute straightforwardness of its appeal and by the singleness of
> its purpose[138]

with similar passages in *Chance*, or with an extract from a letter to Mrs Sanderson which he wrote in 1917:

> The naval training has a peculiar quality, and forms a very fine
> type. For one thing it is strictly methodized to a very definite end
> which is noble in itself and of a very high idealistic nature, while on
> its technical side it deals with a body of systematized facts which
> cannot be questioned as to their value. . . .

In 'The Secret Sharer' the reflection is profoundly ironic, coming as it does immediately before the appearance of Leggatt, who presents the most 'disquieting problems' it is possible to imagine. For the Conrad of the early works the 'strictly methodized' and 'highly idealistic' sea life is no defence against the recognition of the presence of the secret sharer. The virtues which it fosters are unable to deal with Mr Kurtz or with the dilemma of Captain Whalley. But there is no irony in such references in *Chance* or the later letters. It is in this context that we must think of Conrad's idealization of naval life after he had become a public figure. It is not enough to see it merely as an ageing man's nostalgia for the life he had led as a young man nor as a romanticization for the newspaper public. Rather is it an inevitable result of this turning away from the pre-occupations of the works before 'The Secret Sharer'.

I prefer to restrict speculation on the significance of this story's coming soon after he had finished that plunge into his own Polish past which took shape—carefully edited, as all Conrad's reminiscences are—in *A Personal Record*, and while he was writing *Under Western Eyes*, in which his feelings about his early life under the Tsarist tyranny are clearly involved. It is possible that by such speculation we could construct plausible and even correct theories about his feelings concerning his childhood and adolescence, but it would help us little in the task of evaluating his work. What we are concerned with is the presence of a crisis within the works, and of the existence of this there can be little doubt.

There seems to have been within him a continual war between the recognition of the 'heart of darkness' and the desire to rest securely on unquestioned values. His letters tend to show that the desire for security was the more conscious, but in the best of the early works the 'other self' cannot be denied. We have seen something of the struggle emerging in the flaws and insufficiencies of parts of *Lord Jim*. With 'The Secret Sharer' Conrad seems to resolve this conflict for his peace of mind, and we must now consider the works which follow it.

CHAPTER VII

Under Western Eyes and *The Secret Agent*

THE first work completed after 'The Secret Sharer' was *Under Western Eyes*, which Conrad finished in January, 1910. The title is a significant one; the narrator is an English teacher of languages in Geneva who comes in contact there with many Russian émigrés, but who, in the opening pages, denies his competence to tell the story because he has 'no comprehension of the Russian character'. This is clearly not intended to be taken merely as a modest and ironical disclaimer, for it is repeated in varying forms throughout the book in contexts which show that the teacher speaks for Conrad himself.

> I will only remark here [he says a little later], that this is not a story of the West of Europe . . . It is unthinkable that any young Englishman should find himself in Razumov's situation. This being so it would be a vain enterprise to imagine what he would think. The only safe surmise to make is that he would not think as Mr Razumov thought at this crisis of his fate.[139]

This inability of Western minds fully to understand and sympathize with Russian characteristics and motives is what the language teacher stresses more than anything else. Russia is unlike the West:

> In its pride of numbers, in its strange pretensions of sanctity, and in the secret readiness to abase itself in suffering, the spirit of Russia is the spirit of cynicism. It informs the declarations of statesmen, the theories of her revolutionaries, and the mystic vaticinations of prophets to the point of making freedom look like a form of debauch, and the Christian virtues themselves appear actually indecent.[140]

We have already noted that Conrad makes use of his narrators in a number of different ways, and it is quite clear that the teacher of languages resembles the Marlow of

Chance rather than the Marlow of 'Heart of Darkness'. He is not personally involved in the fate of Razumov; nothing new in his own character is brought to the surface by his knowledge of the Russian's treachery and remorse. Nor is he another Captain Mitchell, whose naïve optimism stands ironically in contrast to our deeper knowledge of the real issues of *Nostromo*. Whatever irony is directed against him is very mild. A hint of it—but no more—is implied in a phrase like 'my mind, the decent mind of an old teacher of languages'.[141] There is a certain fussiness about him but there is no indication that his incomprehension is a personal inadequacy, because there is no deeper knowledge against which to measure it. There is no view *sub specie aeternitatis* to compare with the view under western eyes. There can be no doubt that Conrad is in general agreement with his judgments. And it is strange to find the creator of Mr Kurtz, the explorer of the tangle of idealisms and basenesses of *Nostromo*, underwriting such statements as:

> ... this is a Russian story for Western ears, which, as I have observed already, are not attuned to certain tones of cynicism and cruelty, of moral negation and even of moral distress already silenced at our end of Europe[142]

or:

> ... this narrative where the aspects of honour and shame are remote from the ideas of the Western world[143]

The division of mankind into the camp of the good and the camp of the bad, which I have indicated as one of the characteristics on Conrad's later work, is seen here in a special form. The morass of mistaken loyalties, tyranny, deception and shame is, we are constantly informed, a particularly Russian phenomenon. To a great extent, in fact, evil is given a local habitation and a name in Russia. The emphasis throughout is that we—the West—are not tainted by this form of evil. The possessor of the western eyes of the title sees, a little uncomprehendingly, the strange torments of the Russian conscience and the Russian guilt,

G

and we share with him his sense of 'enormous remoteness
from their captivity within the sombre horizon of Russian
problems.'[144]

The subject of Russia was one which engaged Conrad's
feelings most violently. In letters he gives free rein to his
hatred in such remarks as: 'Russians who (nobody would
believe me in 1914) are born rotten'.* He speaks in a different tone in the 'Author's Note' to the Collected Edition,
however, of

> The obligation of absolute fairness . . . imposed on me historically
> and hereditarily, by the peculiar experience of race and family . . .

The repression of Poland by Tsarist Russia—a repression
felt so strongly by the landowning gentry to which Conrad's
family belonged—and the exile and death of his parents
were sufficient to excuse almost any bitterness, and his
realization of the need to overcome it stirs our admiration;
but we cannot feel that he achieves the detachment which
would be necessary before he could treat the subject of
Russian bureaucracy and tyranny in a work of art.

It is not our task to reproach him with intolerance, but
it is essential that we should see the significance of this lack
of detachment. His animus against Russia—his belief that
it is fundamentally more evil than the rest of Europe—
has been introduced into the novel as it stands in his mind
and not subjected to any process of imaginative re-creation.
There is, as a result, an incalculable and incomprehensible
quality in any evaluation of motives and characters—
Russianness.

The minor characters are dealt with very much from
the outside; the comment in the 'Author's Note', though
written some years after the book, catches the spirit in which
they are conceived: 'Peter Ivanovitch and Madame de S.
are fair game. They are the apes of a sinister jungle and are
treated as their grimaces deserve'.

Razumov, however, is treated differently; we see the

* From a letter to Sir Sidney Colvin, 12 November, 1917.

world, for a good deal of the book, through his eyes and, whatever Conrad may do later, in the first part he cannot take up towards him an attitude such as he does towards Peter Ivanovitch or Julius Laspara or any of the other revolutionists. He cannot be merely a 'flat' character, a person in a drama whom we see acting upon others but into whose mind we cannot enter, for he is presented as the point upon which are focused the moral issues and the pressures of Russian society which are Conrad's theme.* Yet the effect of many passages—and especially of those dealing with Razumov's walk through the streets after Haldin has asked for shelter, and his conversation with Haldin before the latter goes out to be arrested—is that of melodrama, over-written and exaggerated. 'His forehead broke out in perspiration while a cold shudder ran down his spine'—'A leaden sleep closed his eyelids at once'—'Sudden fear sealed Razumov's lips'; clichés like these betray the essential unreality of Razumov's plight. The whole passage, especially in Razumov's obsessional dwelling on details like 'the power of goggle eyes and grey whiskers'[145] is heavily indebted to Dostoevsky. And we are asked, in effect, to accept this melodrama as part of a 'Russianness' which we cannot understand, as part of the 'generous indignations and . . . extreme sentiments, too poignant, perhaps, for a non-Russian mind to conceive'.[146] Our inability to form a concrete and deeply realized picture of Razumov's mind is to be seen as a positive success. We are not asked to understand; we can only join the narrator in his uncomprehending observation in what he calls 'my character of a mute witness of things Russian, unrolling their Eastern logic under my Western eyes'.[147]

One of the most obvious characteristics of this work is Conrad's use of irony—more especially the irony of situation. This is brought about, as it is in *Nostromo*, by the

---

* See letter to John Galsworthy, 6 January, 1908: 'I think that I am trying to capture the very soul of things Russian—*Cosas de Russia.*'

arrangement of the sections of the story, by the breaking of the chronological sequence of events. But the effect achieved is very different from that of *Nostromo*. In that book we know, for instance, that the idealism of Charles Gould and his wife will lead eventually to the coming of the chairman of the railway company and his triumphant proclamation of the success of material values. We therefore consider every manifestation of the Goulds' idealism with a deeper knowledge; a criticism of their motives is enforced by our knowledge of the results which are to come. In *Under Western Eyes* we find the opposite process of arrangement at work. We know from the first part what has happened to Haldin and what have been the actions of Razumov, and during the rest of the book we listen to the utterances of people who do not. The irony which results is typified by Natalia Haldin's repetition of her brother's description of Razumov as one of the 'unstained, lofty, and solitary existences',[148] and Sophia Antonovna's: 'You are feeding on some bitterness of your own'.[149]

The difference is fundamental. The method of *Under Western Eyes* does not make the issues any clearer; it enforces no judgments which have not already been made. There is, indeed, something rather heavy and repetitive about a good deal of Parts Two and Three. The narrator is seen as constantly groping towards knowledge which is already in our possession and, since its effect on him is not of importance, since it leads to nothing but horror and incomprehension, no fruitful effect is achieved by such passages as:

> He stared at me so queerly that I hardly know how to define his aspect. I could not understand it in this connexion at all. What ailed him? I asked myself. What strange thought had come into his head? What vision of all the horrors that can be seen in his hopeless country had come suddenly to haunt his brain? If it were anything connected with the fate of Victor Haldin, then I hoped earnestly he would keep it to himself for ever.[150]

§

It is instructive to compare *Under Western Eyes* with *The Secret Agent*, another story of revolutionists and conspirators told in a predominantly ironic temper, which was completed three and a half years before, in September, 1906. This has usually been judged to be different from the majority of Conrad's work, but the difference is on the surface—it is a difference of presentation rather than of the preoccupations which lie at the back of it. There is no central character in whom the problems of value are worked out, no character who is the focal point of the moral issues involved. It is more nearly a comedy than any other novel of Conrad—a comedy which is intensely serious and in which the pity and scorn of which he speaks in the 'Author's Note' are most important. The element of brutal and sordid farce which we have seen in 'Heart of Darkness' and 'Falk' is here dominant.

In describing it in a letter to Ambrose J. Barker on 1 September, 1923, he says: 'My object, apart from the aim of telling a story, was to hold up the worthlessness of certain individuals and the baseness of some others'. In so far as this gives the impression that his attack is confined to certain specific characters in the novel he does his work less than justice. The whole book is conceived in an ironical temper; he describes it very accurately in a letter to R. B. Cunninghame Graham of 7 October, 1907, as 'a sustained effort in ironical treatment of a melodramatic subject'.

We quickly accept the comic note as applied to Mr Verloc; the first few pages establish it by such phrases as 'He breakfasted in bed and remained wallowing there with an air of quiet enjoyment till noon every day'[151] and 'His big, prominent eyes were not well adopted to winking. They were rather of the sort that closes solemnly in slumber with majestic effect'[152] and: 'Mr Verloc, steady like a rock— a soft kind of rock—marched now along a street which

could with every propriety be described as private'.[153]
We move without effort to a similar treatment of the other
conspirators, to Michaelis who 'opened his short, thick
arms, as if in a pathetically hopeless attempt to embrace a
self-regenerated universe',[154] or Ossipon, 'author of a popular quasi-medical study (in the form of a cheap pamphlet
seized promptly by the police) entitled *The Corroding Vices
of the Middle Classes*'.[155]

But the irony does not stop short at the revolutionaries,
the obvious villains; it is extended to their opponents. We
may pass over Chief Inspector Heat's phrasing, when he
asserts that 'none of our lot' has anything to do with the
Greenwich explosion, but when he compares anarchists
with thieves his standard of values is made clearer:

> he could understand the mind of a burglar, because, as a matter of fact,
> the mind and the instincts of a burglar are of the same kind as the mind
> and the instincts of a police officer. Both recognize the same con-
> ventions, and have a working knowledge of each other's methods
> and of the routine of their respective trades. They understand each
> other, which is advantageous to both, and establishes a sort of amenity
> in their relations . . . And Chief Inspector Heat, arrested within six
> paces of the anarchist nicknamed the Professor, gave a thought of
> regret to the world of thieves—sane, without morbid ideals, working
> by routine, respectful of constituted authorities, free from all taint of
> hate and despair.[156]

He speaks to the Professor as to a professional criminal
'perfectly proper words, within the tradition and suitable
to his character of a police officer addressing one of his
special flock'. 'But', we are told, 'the reception they got
departed from tradition and propriety'.[157] The Professor
does not recognize his place in the scheme of closely-knit
relations between the police and the criminal:

> The encounter [Heat feels afterwards], did not leave behind . . .
> that satisfactory sense of superiority the members of the police force
> get from the unofficial but intimate side of their intercourse with the
> criminal classes, by which the vanity of power is soothed, and the
> vulgar love of domination over our fellow-creatures is flattered as
> worthily as it deserves.[158]

He yearns for the days when his duty was to catch thieves, an activity which has 'that quality of seriousness belonging to every form of open sport where the best man wins under perfectly comprehensible rules'.[159]*

It is through the professional worldly wisdom of Heat that the attack is further widened. He explains to the Assistant Commissioner that he can provide sufficient evidence against Michaelis:

> 'You may trust me for that, sir', he added, quite unnecessarily, out of the fullness of his heart; for it seemed to him an excellent thing to have that man in hand to be thrown down to the public should it think fit to roar with any special indignation in this case. It was impossible to say yet whether it would roar or not. That in the last instance depended, of course, on the newspaper press.[160]

This harks back to a passage a few pages earlier which describes the circumstances under which Michaelis was condemned to prison for assisting in the attempted release of some anarchist prisoners, during which, by accident, a police constable was shot:

> the death of that man aroused throughout the length and breadth of a realm for whose defence, welfare, and glory men die every day as matter of duty, an outburst of furious indignation, of a raging, implacable pity for the victim. Three ringleaders got hanged.[161]

Thomas Mann, in his introduction to the German translation of Conrad's works, published in 1926, sees an emphasis in this novel on the contrast between England and Russia and says that the satire against Russian methods comes from a great pride in England's liberty and civilization. It is certainly true that here the English government produces no Mr Vladimirs and that the people of the Embassy deplore the humanitarian bias of the English authorities and people. But Sir Ethelred, the representative of the British government, and his adoring Toodles are not exempted from a scrutiny of less obvious flaws. In particular,

* It is, perhaps, worth remarking that Mr Graham Greene's heavy debt to this novel is nowhere more apparent than in the derivatives from Chief Inspector Heat.

that desire for clear-cut issues, that hope of reducing life to a game with definite rules which is so marked a characteristic of Chief Inspector Heat is also found in the great Sir Ethelred. Nowhere is this more neatly expressed than in his conversation with the Assistant Commissioner:

> 'However' [the Assistant Commissioner is saying], 'this is an imperfect world——'
> The deep-voiced presence on the hearthrug, motionless, with big elbows stuck out, said hastily:
> 'Be lucid, please'.[162]

It is this difference in the scope and function of the irony which marks the real distinction between *Under Western Eyes* and *The Secret Agent*. *Under Western Eyes* has some excellent qualities, and *The Secret Agent* some obvious weaknesses (the exposition of the Professor's theories, for example, leans heavily on Dostoevsky's treatment of nihilism but suffers in its lack of subtlety from the comparison); but the fundamental difference between the two works is that all the characters and all the beliefs of *The Secret Agent* are presented in the same ironical mood, whereas in *Under Western Eyes* there is an implied 'Western' code of behaviour which escapes investigation.

The irony of *The Secret Agent*, and of other early works in which it is less pervasive, is *offensive*; it is a weapon to undermine comfortable assumptions and to make us scrutinize more deeply our beliefs and values. In the later works it is normally *defensive*, in that—like the constant references to Peter Ivanovitch as 'the heroic fugitive' and 'the greatest of feminists'—it underlines an obvious sneer at a deliberately 'unsympathetic' character, or acts as a shield for personal intrusions, cutting short investigation by the striking of an attitude. The whole of *The Secret Agent* is conceived in an ironical temper. In works like *The Rover* and *Chance* irony is used intermittently and does not exclude a totally uncritical worship of sentimentally conceived characters and attitudes.

CHAPTER VIII

Chance

Chance was published in 1913, but Conrad had been long writing it. Begun towards the end of 1906, it was laid aside (because it did not develop as he wished) while he wrote *Under Western Eyes*, *A Personal Record*, 'The Secret Sharer' and a number of less important short stories; and it was then taken up again in the summer of 1910 and finished in March, 1912. It belongs, that is, to the period of crisis and change in Conrad's writing life which I have seen as epitomized in 'The Secret Sharer'.

It was with this novel that Conrad first achieved popular success, and it always remained one of his own favourites,* but it bears, more clearly than *Under Western Eyes*, the marks of the decline in his art, the disappearance of those qualities which give such power to 'Heart of Darkness' and *Nostromo*.

It may be objected that in formulating this judgment I am laying *Chance* on a Procrustean bed or blaming Conrad for not rewriting the early books again and again. But it seems plain that the later works, in general, show a retreat from the degree of awareness of the complexity of human emotion found in the early ones. The division of mankind into the camp of the good and the camp of the bad, for instance, is clearly a sign of a restriction rather than a change of interest.

The obvious flaws of *Chance*—its clichés, its defensive irony, its imprecise rhetoric—can be seen to come, I believe, from this evasion of the painful awareness of the darker side of even our good feelings. His theme here is, ostensibly, very much like those of the works we have already

---

* Cf. letter to J. B. Pinker, 2 June, 1913: 'As to what *it is*, I am very confident . . . One doesn't do a trick like that twice'.

examined, the study of 'the utter falseness of his [Anthony's], I may say, aspirations, the vanity of grasping the empty air'.[163] But in fact the investigation is never undertaken. Too much is exempted from the scrutiny.

§

The two parts of the novel are entitled 'The Damsel' and 'The Knight'. No better example could be found for the statement at the end of my last chapter, that in his later works Conrad's irony is normally defensive. These are, fairly obviously, ironic titles; this, we are to infer, is how Anthony sees the situation; we have been told that he inherited an excessive tendency towards the conception of chivalry from his father. But it is also, at bottom, how Conrad sees it, and the irony is intended to defend him against the suspicion of not having realized how over-simplified and falsely romantic is his treatment of the plight of his characters.

The deep misunderstanding between Anthony and his wife is symbolized in previously unheard-of cabin arrangements. The projection of inner states in outer phenomena is effected with all Conrad's usual consistency. One example alone is enough to show his thoroughness: when the ship is in danger young Powell stamps on the deck to summon the captain, but Anthony and his wife do not share a cabin and so he is not warned in time of the danger to his command. There is, indeed, a great deal of emphasis throughout the scenes on board the *Ferndale* on the potential danger to the whole ship's company until the false situation is resolved. In this there is a distinct resemblance to 'The Secret Sharer'. But the situation of the main characters—of Anthony and Flora—is far different from that of the narrator of the short story. Here we find no haunting feeling of guilt, but a misunderstanding caused by Anthony's excess of chivalrous delicacy acting upon that morbid sensitiveness with which

Flora has been affected as the result of horrible experiences in her childhood and youth.

She, the damsel, is one of Conrad's repeated characters. He continually recurs in his later works to the figure of the woman of superlative purity and beauty, smirched by a world which is too gross or evil for her: Rita de Lastaola in *The Arrow of Gold*, Adèle de Montevesso in *Suspense*, Arlette Réal in *The Rover*. We may reasonably suppose that the original of Rita de Lastaola—the woman with whom he was in love in his early gun-running days in Marseilles and for whom he fought a duel—is the original of them all.

The experiences which have scarred Flora's mind are entirely the fault of people depicted either—like the Fynes—as unable to understand her needs because of theoretical preconceptions, or—like the governess and the uncle—as totally evil or despicable. It should be noted that the governess is not described merely as an ordinarily selfish and vindictive woman. Conrad's preoccupation with evil is in evidence here, as in 'Heart of Darkness', but the evil is restricted to some characters; Flora bears none of it within herself.

> The girl was astounded and alarmed [he says] by the altogether unknown expression in the woman's face. The stress of passion often discloses an aspect of the personality completely ignored till then by its closest intimates. There was something like an emanation of evil from her eyes and from the face of the other, who, exactly behind her and overtopping her by half a head, kept his eyelids lowered in a sinister fashion...[164]

Flora has been hurt by the world before she is old enough to have developed weapons against it. It has taught her fear, humiliation, despair, a 'poisoned sleep', until she has 'a spirit neither made cringing nor yet dulled but as if bewildered in quivering hopelessness by gratuitous cruelty ... The passive anguish of the luckless!'[165] But it has taught her neither calculation nor evil.

Anthony, the knight, is presented chiefly through the adoring eyes of Powell or through the medium of Marlow's reminiscences, and he, too, is something of a stock character. Clearly he is far too good for this world and he is described continually in the most romantic terms. He paces the deck with his eyes averted with 'the tenderness of silent solitary men',[166] at sea, where 'you hear no tormenting echoes of your own littleness . . . where either a great elemental voice roars defiantly under the sky or else an elemental silence seems to be part of the infinite stillness of the universe'.[167] He has 'native rectitude, sea-salted, hardened in the winds of wide horizons, open as the day'.[168] He is summed up thus:

> Solitude had been his best friend. He wanted some place where he could sit down and be alone. And in his need his thoughts turned to the sea which had given him so much of that congenial solitude. There, if always with his ship (but that was an integral part of him) he could always be as solitary as he chose. Yes. Get out to sea![169]

What there is in this book of that profound and searching investigation of human nature and beliefs which we find in Conrad's best early work is vague and offset at once by rhetoric. From time to time Marlow throws out dark hints of qualities in Anthony to which he cannot give his unstinted and rapturous admiration, but the hints are always couched in terms which lead us rather to admire than to explore.

> I am convinced [he says] that he used reading as an opiate against the pain of his magnanimity which, like all abnormal growths, was gnawing at his healthy substance with cruel persistence.[170]

He discusses how far the element of vanity entered into Anthony's motives:

> The inarticulate son had set up a standard for himself with that need for embodying in his conduct the dreams, the passion, the impulses the poet puts into arrangements of verses, which are dearer to him than his own self—and may make his own self appear sublime in the eyes of other people, and even in his own eyes.
> Did Anthony wish to appear sublime in his own eyes? I should not

like to make that charge . . . I do not even think that there was in
what he did a conscious and lofty confidence in himself, a particularly
pronounced sense of power which leads men so often into impossible
or equivocal situations.[171]

This, coming after the comment that his father's standards
of delicacy had worn out two women, might suggest closer
investigation of all Anthony's motives, were it not that
the passage closes with yet another gesture of adoration
before the idealized figure:

. . . this eager appropriation was truly the act of a man of solitude
and desire; a man also, who, unless a complete imbecile, must have
been a man of long and ardent reveries wherein the faculty of sincere
passion matures slowly in the unexplored recesses of the heart.[172]

There is one section of the book where it seems that we
are moving towards that kind of criticism, that ruthless
investigation of the sources and nature of our feelings,
which is Conrad's special power. Marlow, describing his
talk with Flora outside the East End pub, has remarked
of Flora's letter to Mrs Fyne:

What a sell these confessions are! What a horrible sell! You seek
sympathy, and all you get is the most evanescent sense of relief—
if you get that much. For a confession, whatever it may be, stirs the
secret depths of the hearer's character. Often depths that he himself is
but dimly aware of.[173]

He goes on to recount Flora's story of how Anthony
declared his love. She says that, walking with her, he was
'following her with an air of extreme interest. Interest or
eagerness? At any rate she caught an expression on his face
which frightened her'. A little later, after he has seen how
miserable she is, we are told that:

What seemed most awful to her was the elated light in his eyes, the
rapacious smile that would come and go as if he were gloating over
her misery. But her misery was his opportunity and he rejoiced
while the tenderest pity seemed to flood his whole being . . . the very
marks and stamp of this ill-usage of which he was so certain seemed
to add to the inexplicable attraction he felt for her person . . . It gave
him the feeling that if only he could get hold of her, no woman would
belong to him so completely as this woman.[174]

He asks her to come down to him in the garden, and the thought comes to her 'that should he get into ungovernable fury from disappointment and perchance strangle her, it would be as good a way to be done with it as any'.

Marlow comments:

> This makes one shudder at the mysterious way girls acquire knowledge. For this was a thought, wild enough, I admit, but which could only have come from the depths of that sort of experience which she had not had, and went far beyond a young girl's possible conception of the strongest and most veiled of human emotions.[175]

But, she says, 'He was gentleness itself', and the edge of this perception of a possible darker side to Anthony's passion is blunted; the criticism is directed away from him and left as a general reflection on human nature from which the tone of the prose seems to except him, and before long we find such passages, typical of Marlow's descriptions of Anthony, as:

> . . . the desire of that man to whom the sea and sky of his solitary life had appeared suddenly incomplete without that glance which seemed to belong to them both—[176]

the glance, that is, of Flora's eyes—and he is telling her 'that to be fair you must trust a man altogether—or not at all', and summing up Anthony as *'un galant homme'*. The section ends with Anthony as

> the son of the poet, the rescuer of the most forlorn damsel of modern times, the man of violence, gentleness and generosity.[177]

The same hint of criticism is seen in Marlow's perception at the climax of the events on board the *Ferndale*:

> . . . if two beings thrown together, mutually attracted, resist the necessity, fail in understanding and voluntarily stop short of the— the embrace, in the noblest meaning of the word, then they are committing a sin against life, the call of which is simple. Perhaps sacred. And the punishment of it is an invasion of complexity, a tormenting, forcibly tortuous involution of feelings.[178]

But there is no attempt to show any inherent inadequacy in Anthony; there is no suggestion of any deep inhibition of feeling in him. The 'involution' is entirely a temporary matter—a matter of this particular situation. As soon as Anthony and Flora realize that they are in a false position, all can be well.

Despite these few hints of Marlow, then, a highly romanticized figure is presented to us, a man with no flaw but his overdeveloped delicacy; and from this flaw proceeds, for Flora, 'this new perfidy of life taking upon itself the form of magnanimity'. The situation is summed up in a comment on Marlow:

> In the full light of the room I saw in his eyes that slightly mocking expression with which he habitually covers up his sympathetic impulses of mirth and pity before *the unreasonable complications the idealism of mankind puts into the simple but poignant problem of conduct on this earth.*[179]*

We are required to believe in an unbelievably fine man so as to be shown the harm that comes from the over-development of one virtue. But we are not convinced of the reality of the man, nor, therefore, of the significance of the central situation. In place of the interaction of a complexity of motives in which what seems good is ironically linked with bad, such as we find in *Nostromo* or *The Secret Agent* or 'The End of the Tether', we are presented with a misunderstanding—a 'false situation', in Marlow's words, arising from an excess of a virtue. The effect can, perhaps, be summed up by saying that we are sure that at a number of points in the story the most natural remark (the most natural remark, that is, even of these two inhibited characters) would end the whole misunderstanding. We do not feel it to be 'chance', and the previous histories of Conrad's personages which prolong the intolerably false position, but the guiding hand of the story-teller. By contrast with *Nostromo*, where the progress of 'material interests' and the idealism and fidelity of Charles Gould lead inevitably to

* My italics.

every disaster and every apparent triumph, the issues in *Chance* stand out as contrived.

De Barral ('Mr Smith') finally resolves the situation by trying to poison Anthony. Throughout the greater part of the book de Barral is treated as one of the 'apes of a sinister jungle'. In the earlier sections, however, where Marlow reminisces on his financial schemes and his trial, there is some description of his 'air of placid sufficiency which was the first hint to the world of the man's over-weening, unmeasurable conceit, hidden hitherto under a diffident manner'. But Conrad appears to be little interested in creating the man himself—only in showing the dirtiness of finance which is contrasted throughout the book with the cleanness of the sea—and this perfunctoriness seems to be admitted in the description of Flora and her father walking hand in hand: 'Figures from Dickens—pregnant with pathos'.[180] Once brought to the heart of the story, he is a man apart. Marlow, speaking of his release from prison, says:

> And the release! . . . How do they do it? Pull the string, door flies open, man flies through: Out you go! Adios! And in the space where a second before you were not, in the silent space there is a figure going away, limping. Why limping? I don't know. That's how I see it. One has a notion of a maiming, crippling process; of the individual coming back damaged in some subtle way.[181]

He is maimed, he is the *diabolus ex machina*, and there is no possible contact between him and Anthony. We remember the connection in the earlier works between the man who is supposedly above reproach and the 'bad' man whom he cannot disown: Lord Jim and Gentleman Brown, Marlow and Kurtz. The dénouement in these books comes from the realization of similarities between men apparently dissimilar and of the complexity of human character, of the 'unforeseen partnership'. But here de Barral leads to no further knowledge of Anthony, who could never under-stand his father-in-law because he is himself presented as immune from all evil but his one excess of chivalry, as 'the man ... of silence made only more impressive by the inarticulate thunders and mutters of the great seas, an utter stranger to the clatter of tongues.'[182]

Once the misunderstanding is removed, therefore, there is nothing left to prevent Anthony and Flora living together in perfect happiness and goodness—save that (presumably for the sake of the 'shape' of the story) Anthony has to be perfunctorily drowned and Flora given to Powell.

Conrad's tone is especially idealizing and romantic in the scene where Anthony and Flora, for the first time, understand one another's love.[183] Clichés abound: Anthony has 'a glance full of unwonted fire', he clasps Powell's shoulder 'as if in a vice', Flora is 'whiter than the lilies'. Irony, serving no such purpose as the irony of *The Secret Agent*, is there in:

> She looked as if she would let go and sink to the floor if the captain were to withhold his sustaining arm. But the captain obviously had no such intention.

Evil is something external which can be removed and Conrad's tone of surrender to his own idealized creations is complete.

But the 'shape' of the book demands that Anthony shall die and that Powell shall be sent at the end to claim his widow. The obvious concern for structure is probably the most immediately striking thing about the novel. It drew from Henry James the praise:

> It places Mr Conrad absolutely alone as a votary of the way to do a thing that shall make it undergo most doing ... What concerns us is that the general effect of *Chance* is arrived at by a pursuance of means to the end in view contrasted with every other current form of the chase can only affect us as cheap and futile.[184]

It would seem that *Chance* shows the influence of James' own work more than any other of Conrad's books and this is most obvious in the manipulation of the plot. The bringing together of Flora and Anthony and their presentation

H

through the Fynes reminds us at once of James' beloved indirect method, and it is excellently done. But this technique does seem at times to be there for its own sake. We may sympathize, I feel, with those critics, against whom Conrad defended himself in the 'Author's Note', who asked whether it could not all have been done more simply.

Why, we have a right to ask, do we have the long—and (in itself) excellent—opening section, the loving reconstruction of a sailor's feelings when he gets his first post as an officer? Our need to understand Powell, who will be our chief source of information about life on the *Ferndale*, hardly demands as much as this.

I have already emphasized* that in *Nostromo*, where shifts in time and viewpoint are also common, they enforce criticisms and judgments. But in *Chance* they rarely serve such a function and there is no such sustained investigation of human motives and actions depending on them. Most clearly of all, we cannot see the casual killing of Anthony— almost an afterthought from Powell—as anything but arbitrary and wanton. The love of a good 'shape' is the only possible reason and this 'shape' is external; it arises from no inner organization or necessity; it is in no way connected with the spiritual and psychological issues involved.

It is interesting to note that James' praise, part of which I have quoted, is very qualified. One of his conclusions is:

> It literally strikes us that his volume sets in motion more than any-thing else a drama in which his own system and his combined eccentricities of recital represent the protagonist in face of powers leagued against it, and of which the dénouement gives us the system fighting in triumph, though with its back desperately to the wall, and laying the powers piled up at its feet. This frankly has been *our* spectacle, our suspense and our thrill; with the one flaw on the roundness of it all the fact that the predicament was not imposed rather than invoked, was not the effect of a challenge from without, but that of a mystic impulse from within.'

The chief means by which the story is presented to us,

* Chapter V, pp. 66–69.

however, and that which gives it the 'richness' which has
so often been found in it, is the commentary of Marlow.
Throughout the work he compares, philosophizes, muses.
He is not, as in 'Heart of Darkness', fundamentally affected
by what happens. He is the commentator and his comments
are clearly intended to be those of the reader. But what
are they?

We find such reflections as:

> You expect a cogency of conduct not usual in women . . . the
> subterfuges of a menaced passion are not to be fathomed,[185]

or:

> You say I don't know women. Maybe. It's just as well not to come
> too close to the shrine. But I have a clear notion of *woman*. In all of
> them, termagant, flirt, crank, washerwoman, bluestocking, outcast
> and even in the ordinary fool of the ordinary commerce there is
> something left, if only a spark. And when there is a spark there can
> always be a flame . . . [186]

[the aposiopesis is Marlow's] or:

> And even in the best armour of steel there are joints a treacherous
> stroke can always find if chance gives the opportunity.[187]

It seems unlikely that such a commentator will reveal
to us much of significance. The large generalizations, the
clichés, the vague rhetorical outbursts which we found from
time to time in *Lord Jim* are normal here.

It is often difficult to see the relevance of his comments
either to the facts of the story he tells or to any deeper logic
of mood. We find in close succession in Part I, Chapter II:

> It was one of those dewy, clear, starry nights, oppressing our spirit,
> crushing our pride, by the brilliant evidence of the awful loneliness,
> of the hopeless obscure insignificance of our globe lost in the splendid
> revelation of a glittering soulless universe. I hate such skies.

and

> I . . . went out of the cottage to be confronted outside its door
> by the bespangled, cruel revelation of the Immensity of the Universe.

and

> . . . it was a fine day; a delicious day, with the horror of the Infinite
> veiled by the splendid tent of blue.

A passage right at the end of the book stands in striking contrast to these:

> The amenity of a fine day in its decline surrounded me with a beneficent, a calming influence; I felt it in the silence of the shady lane, in the pure air, in the blue sky. It is difficult to retain the memory of the conflicts, miseries, temptations and crimes of men's self-seeking existence when one is alone with the charming serenity of the unconscious nature. Breathing the dreamless peace around the picturesque cottage I was approaching, it seemed to me that it must reign everywhere, over all the globe of water and land and in the hearts of all the dwellers on this earth.[188]

It would, no doubt, be too naïve to ask that Marlow should have either one view of Nature or the other. What I am suggesting is that he can move from one to the other so easily because neither is very real. The 'Immensity of the Universe', the 'charming serenity', 'the dreamless peace around the picturesque cottage'—these are no more than rhetoricians' properties and Marlow expresses himself in the most hackneyed clichés because it is at that level that he is thinking.

But Marlow reserves most of his vague generalizations and purple patches for the subject of women. He frequently combines a rather obvious irony—'The pluck of women! The optimism of the dear creatures'—with a tone of rapt adoration:

> Man, we know, cannot live by bread alone, but hang me if I don't believe that some women could live by love alone. If there be a flame in human beings fed by varied ingredients earthly and spiritual which tinge it in different hues, then I seem to see the colour of theirs.[189]

Again and again he emphasizes in general terms the mysteriousness of women.

> A young girl [he says] is something like a temple. You pass by and wonder what mysterious rites are going on in there, what prayers, what visions? The privileged men, the lover, the husband, who are given the key of the sanctuary do not always know how to use it.[190]

Again:

> Flora de Barral was not exceptionally intelligent but she was
> thoroughly feminine. She would be passive (and that does not mean
> inanimate) in *the circumstances, where the mere fact of being a woman was
> enough to give her an occult and supreme significance.*[191]*

From time to time he defends himself from being an
unreliable judge of women with a heavy irony, as in such a
passage as:

> For myself it's towards women that I feel vindictive mostly, in my
> small way . . . Mainly I resent that pretence of winding us round their
> dear little fingers, as of right . . . It is the assumption that each of us is
> a combination of a kid and an imbecile which I find provoking—
> in a small way; in a very small way. You needn't stare as though
> I were breathing fire and smoke out of my nostrils. I am not a woman-
> devouring monster. I am not even what is technically called 'a brute'.
> I hope there's enough of a kid and an imbecile in me to answer the
> requirements of some really good woman eventually—some day . . .
> Some day.[192]

But there is no irony directed against him. There can be no
doubt that his comments are supposed to have our approval.
Yet they are not ones which can lay bare any profound
moral or psychological or spiritual issues; they exist rather
to cast a haze of romance and mystery over certain aspects
of his theme.

The sea and the sea-captain, too, are continually looked
at through this mist of rhetoric. The two are linked:

> It's true the sea is an uncertain element, but no sailor remembers
> this in the presence of its bewitching power any more than a lover
> ever thinks of the proverbial inconstancy of women . . . the captain
> of a ship at sea is a remote, inaccessible creature, something like a
> prince of a fairy-tale, alone of his kind . . .[193]

Conrad reflects, on the link established between Marlow
and Powell,

> . . . the service of the sea and the service of a temple are both detached
> from the vanities and errors of a world which follows no severe
> rule.[194]

* My italics.

We remember the irony of the narrator's reflections in 'The Secret Sharer' on the simplicity of life at sea, or the voyage of Nostromo and Decoud in the lighter, or even such passages from *The Mirror of the Sea* as: '... the sea that plays with men till their hearts are broken, and wears stout ships to death'. But here, once the intruder—'Mr Smith'—who hates the sea is removed, then indeed 'The sea was there to give them the shelter of its solitude free from the earth's petty suggestions'.[195]

More and more, as Conrad goes on writing, shall we find rhetoric used to make us accept valuations and judgments which have not been as deeply considered as those of his best early work, and already in *Chance* the process is far developed. We find it—even down to a care for sentence inversion—in such a passage as:

> Captain Anthony had not moved away from the taffrail. He remained in the very position he took up to watch the other ship go by rolling and swinging all shadowy in the uproar of the following seas. He stirred not; and Powell keeping near-by did not dare speak to him, so enigmatical in its contemplation of the night did his figure appear to his young eyes: indistinct—and in its immobility staring into gloom, the prey of some incomprehensible grief, longing or regret.[196]

CHAPTER IX

Victory

WHEN we consider its theme, it seems at first that we must exclude *Victory* from our generalization about the change which comes over Conrad's work after 'The Secret Sharer' and that we must attribute any flaws of vague rhetoric or sentimentality, which we will hardly fail to find in it, to some other cause than that retreat from a complex awareness of the mingling of evil and good in human nature and of the untrustworthiness of the ideals which we set up for ourselves. Is not Axel Heyst a man who intends to do good but who brings about evil because altruism is mixed in him with a coldness which is partly his own responsibility, partly an inheritance from his father? As in *Lord Jim*, his self-sought isolation, where he is of supreme importance to those dependent on him, is broken into by the 'envoys extraordinary of the world'[197] with whom he is in 'spectral fellowship'.[198] Though, after the arrival of Mr Jones and his two followers ('a sort of fate—the retribution that waits its time')[199] he feels that

> the sceptical carelessness which had accompanied every one of his attempts at action, like a secret reserve of his soul, fell away from him. He no longer belonged to himself. There was a call far more imperious and august,[200]

yet his 'infernal mistrust of all life'[201] is only finally conquered when it is too late to save Lena, and he is left to say, before killing himself, 'woe to the man whose heart has not learned while young to hope, to love—and to put its trust in life'.[202] Is there not even, it may be asked, a clear resemblance to the earlier works in the awareness of Heyst that the inhuman detachment of Mr Jones is akin to his own?

To these questions we must answer 'Yes'—so long as we

are discussing only a paraphrase of the book, the theme in isolation, an abstraction from the total effect of the work. But we have already seen how inadequate is a paraphrase of Conrad's best works as a statement of their meaning. The invention of a fable which poses a moral problem is neither difficult nor important. It is the embodiment of this theme in a series of concrete situations, in the detailed creation of character, in the flow of the narration and imagery which is significant.* We can only know what precise criticisms of life are offered in, say, *Nostromo* or 'Heart of Darkness' when we study in the greatest detail the interplay of incident, of character and of the words—above all, in Conrad, of the words. Hence I have frequently presented detailed analyses of various passages as a basis for considering his importance as a novelist.

As soon as we begin to give *Victory* this sort of attention we become aware of a discrepancy between the paraphrased theme and the actual effect which the book has on us. Much of this discrepancy centres about Heyst himself, and we are forced to ask ourselves whether the unnatural detachment, the inhibition of feeling which he so bitterly laments in his last words, is ever more than something about which we are told, but which is not created fully and convincingly. The response demanded of us by the language which describes him is quite different from the effect which an outline of the plot would seem to require.

He appears from the first as the object of all Schomberg's hatred and this alone is enough to prejudice us in his favour. Schomberg is a villain of Conrad's later type—a villain, that is, unredeemed by any trace of goodness or even of amiability. Because Heyst patronizes Schomberg's establishment only three times the innkeeper wishes him 'nothing less than a long and tormented existence'; on this Conrad is heavily ironical: 'Observe the Teutonic sense of propor-

---

* I am not, of course, suggesting that this is the chronology of the process of creation for Conrad or, indeed, for any other writer.

tion and nice forgiving temper'.[203] Conrad assures us in
the 'Author's Note' that Schomberg is not the result of
'recent animosities'—the animosities of the war of 1914
which broke out shortly before the novel was published—
and that he is an old member of his company, whose
grotesque psychology is only completed by this book; but
he is, nevertheless, remarkably like a war-time caricature of
the enemy. Conrad's racial prejudices are strong and narrow
and the Alsatian's nationality is insisted upon in such a naïve
description of his anger as:

> He was beside himself in his lurid, heavy, Teutonic manner, so
> unlike the picturesque, lively rage of the Latin races.[204]

Heyst has all the qualities which stand in contrast to his
enemy's baseness. He is presented as a romantic figure—
something, indeed, of a stock character. When Morrison
inveighs in despair against the Portuguese authorities who
have trapped him, Heyst makes 'with his eyebrows, a slight
motion of surprise which would not have been misplaced
in a drawing room',[205] and listens to his story with 'that
consummate good-society manner of his'.[206] 'Native
delicacy' is one of his most notable characteristics and we
are told that 'no decent feeling was ever scorned by Heyst'.[207]

The impression made on the narrator of the first part of
the story by the disappearance of Heyst with Lena reminds
us of the carrying off of Flora de Barral by Captain Anthony
in *Chance*. 'Davidson shared my suspicion', he says, 'that
this was in its essence the rescue of a distressed human
being'.[208] The similarities in the presentation of the two
characters are striking and the effect on the reader is the same
in both cases. Heyst, like Anthony, is shown as a lover of
the silence of lonely places:

> Like most dreamers, to whom it is given sometimes to hear the
> music of the spheres, Heyst, the wanderer of the Archipelago, had a
> taste for silence which he had been able to gratify for years. The islands
> are very quiet. One sees them lying about, clothed in their dark

garments of leaves, in a great hush of silver and azure, where the sea
without murmurs meets the sky in a ring of magic stillness.[209]

This passage follows hard upon one which describes that
detachment from normal human feelings which he is at last
to recognize as a disastrous aberration:

> Heyst was disenchanted with life as a whole. His scornful tempera-
> ment, beguiled into action, suffered from failure in a subtle way un-
> known to men accustomed to grapple with the realities of common
> human enterprise.[210]

The effect of this is that all sense of there being a flaw in his
nature disappears because it is so generally and so vaguely
expressed, and because it is swamped by the response of
admiration which he receives as a man who is in touch with
the beauty and tranquillity of the islands. We feel, rather,
that in some subtle way he is superior to the generality of
men. The impression of Heyst which we form is determined by his rescue of Morrison and of Lena and by his
contrast with Schomberg; it is but little affected by the
generalizations of:

> Heyst was not conscious of either friends or enemies. It was the
> very essence of his life to be a solitary achievement, accomplished not
> by hermit-like withdrawal with its silence and immobility, but by a
> system of restless wandering, by the detachment of an impermanent
> dweller amongst changing scenes. In this scheme he had perceived
> the means of passing through life without suffering and almost with-
> out a single care in the world—invulnerable because elusive.[211]

We see Heyst, therefore, very much as we see Captain
Anthony—as a romantically conceived figure of more than
normal distinction and delicacy of feeling, suffering from a
flaw in which we find it hard to believe. This is certainly
far from the effect which Conrad intended to produce; the
disastrous force of nihilism is undoubtedly a subject which
engaged his deepest feelings.* It is a significant pointer to
his own attitude to the issues involved that he speaks of

---

* Cf. letter to H. S. Canby, 7 April, 1924: 'It is a book in which I have tried
to grasp at more "life-stuff" than perhaps in any other of my works'.

Heyst's father in terms which are very reminiscent of the
Professor in *The Secret Agent*, as

> the man who had spent his life in blowing blasts upon a terrible
> trumpet which had filled heaven and earth with ruins, while mankind
> went on its way unheeding. . . . His son buried the silenced destroyer
> of systems, of hopes, of beliefs, He observed that the death of that
> bitter contemner of life did not trouble the flow of life's stream, where
> men and women go by thick as dust, revolving and jostling one
> another like figures cut out of cork and weighted with lead just
> sufficiently to keep them in their proudly upright posture.[212]

Yet when Heyst says: 'I cared little for life and still less for
death'[213] or:

> 'I, Axel Heyst, the most detached of creatures in this earthly
> captivity, the veriest tramp on this earth, an indifferent stroller going
> through the world's bustle . . . I, a man of universal scorn and un-
> belief. . . .'[214]

we echo Lena's comment: 'You are putting it on'.

But if Heyst's flaw is never made real, if Conrad seems to
remain unable to convince us of any evil in his hero, there
is no lack of villainy in his villains. The tendency which
we have already seen in his work for the good characters to
become better while the bad ones become worse is carried
to its extreme in the sinister trio of Mr Jones, Martin
Ricardo and Pedro. Pedro, 'a simple straightforward
brute, if a murderous one', is the least evil; the other two
suggest 'a stealthy deliberate wild-cat turned into a man'
and 'an insolent spectre on leave from Hades, endowed with
skin and bones and a subtle power of terror'.[215] This is how
they appear to Schomberg, and to Heyst they seem much
the same: 'evil intelligence, instinctive savagery arm in arm.
The brute force is at the back'.[216] The simplified black and
white distinction of good and evil is reinforced as an
objective judgment by the description of Heyst's conversation with Mr Jones in Pedro's presence as 'the conversation
of an evil spectre with a disarmed man, watched by an
ape',[217] while Ricardo, finding Lena, is unable to repress
'the instinct for the feral spring'.

Nothing is omitted that might add to a picture of melo-dramatic wickedness. Mr Jones' appearance, described at some length, is in keeping with his character:

> In repose his features had a curious character of evil, exhausted austerity; but when he smiled, the whole mask took on an un-pleasantly infantile expression.[218]

Later: 'his aspect became still more gruesomely malevolent, as of a wicked and pitiless corpse.[219] When he learns of the presence of a woman on the island, he forgets himself 'to the point of executing a dance of rage in the middle of the floor'.[220] In conversation he recalls his past crimes with a self-conscious and affected casualness:

> Shall I tell you [he asks] how I killed his brother in the wilds of Colombia? Well, perhaps some other time—it's a rather long story[221]

and:

> But we aren't tame. We once kept a whole angry town at bay for two days, and then we got away with our plunder. It was in Venezuela. Ask Martin here—he can tell you.[222]

There is little wonder that when Schomberg finds the fire-arms in their luggage he comes to the rather ingenuously phrased judgment: 'By heavens, they are desperadoes'.

There is one section of the book where Conrad makes more effort to enter into the workings of Ricardo's mind. It is that in which he discovers Lena in the bungalow and it seems that he is to be presented to us as a sadist—in the strict meaning of that much abused term. After his greedy visualization of the 'ripping up' of Heyst, an impulse which is 'so to speak, constitutional', he finds Lena doing her hair in the supposedly deserted room and feels that:

> Ravish or kill—it was all one to him, as long as by the act he liberated the suffering soul of savagery repressed for so long.[223]

But usually it is enough that he should serve as a symbol of a conventional brutality and wickedness which there is no need for us to understand.

It was, perhaps, unfortunate for Conrad that he was writing at a time when literary conventions did not permit him to introduce any strong oaths into his books, for the result of his attempts to convey Ricardo's speech is at times perilously close to the idiom of the schoolboy's adventure story:

> But these Dutchmen aren't any good. They never seem to get warmed up properly, win or lose. I've tried them both ways, too. Hang them for a beggarly, bloodless lot of animated cucumbers![224]

He is, in short, a pasteboard figure overdrawn to the point of caricature. We cannot take seriously a man who speaks thus:

> Aha, dog! This will teach you to keep back where you belong, you murdering brute, you slaughtering savage, you. You infidel, you robber of churches! Next time I will rip you open from neck to heel, you carrion-eater![225]

and thus:

> I think you are mad yet . . . And if I thought you had been to the police, I would tell Pedro to catch you round the waist and break your fat neck by jerking your head backwards—*snap*! I saw him do it to a big buck nigger who was flourishing a razor in front of the governor. It can be done. You hear a low crack, that's all—and the man drops down like a limp rag![226]

Nor does he give a greater impression of reality when he is making love. He is 'literary', though in a slightly different tradition, when he says:

> I went tired this morning, since I came in here and started talking to you—as tired as if I had been pouring my life-blood here on these planks for you to dabble your white feet in.[227]

He is, in fact, what he appears to Lena to be—'the embodied evil of the world'—and this evil is totally external to her, for she is the white to his black. She is, moreover, equally 'literary' in her speech in such passages as:

> They call me Alma. I don't know why. Silly name! Magdalen too. It doesn't matter; you can call me by whatever name you choose. Yes, you give me a name. Think of one you would like the sound of— something quite new. How I should like to forget everything that has gone before, as one forgets a dream that's done with, fright and all! I would try![228]

I am not suggesting that we should condemn Conrad for not
writing all his dialogue with the meticulous attention to
realism of a naturalist. His conversations are often 'literary'
—not only those of Marlow, where no discordant note is
usually felt, but even of such personages as Donkin in *The
Nigger of the 'Narcissus'*. Above all, he can never catch the
note of the uneducated. But what is only a minor flaw in
Donkin is here the index of something more. It is essential
for the effect of the book that we should see Lena as coming
from a background of lodgings off the Kingsland Road,
as having the naïveté of the uneducated waif, and yet as
bringing love and faith to the intellectual and highly
educated Heyst. But she is palpably a creation of the writer
for his scheme and a projection from his romantic conception of woman.

An essential quality of 'Heart of Darkness' and *The Secret
Agent* and *Nostromo* is, as we have seen, that we observe
every person and every motive with the same eyes; we are
allowed to accept nothing simply and without scrutiny.
But here the attitude of Conrad to Lena is manifestly
different from his attitude to Ricardo; she is a heroine,
he is a villain; he is embodied evil, she is flawless. And to
persuade us to accept her at his valuation he lavishes much
rhetoric upon her, rhetoric which produces for the critical
reader the opposite result from what is intended. It abounds
in clichés of which in his best work he could never have
been guilty: 'There was a flash of fire in her mysterious
eyes—a red gleam in the white mist which wrapped the
promptings and longings of her soul'[229] 'every modulation
of her enchanting voice',[230] 'the faint smile on her deep-cut
lips waned, and her head sank deep into the pillow, taking
on the majestic pallor and immobility of marble'.[231]
Above all, the note of surrender is dominant in the pages
which describe her death. This was the only passage from
his work which Conrad, sensitive about his foreign accent,
ever read to an audience—whose 'audible snuffling', as he

said in a letter to his wife, greatly pleased him. But it shows his later writing at its worst. The chapter ends with a surfeit of vague and conventionally potent adjectives and with a rhythm which tries to lull us into uncritical acceptance:

> Exulting, she saw herself extended on the bed, in a black dress, and profoundly at peace; while, stooping over her with a kindly, playful smile, he was ready to lift her up in his firm arms and take her into the sanctuary of his innermost heart—for ever! The flush of rapture flooding her whole being broke out in a smile of innocent, girlish happiness; and with that divine radiance on her lips she breathed her last, triumphant, seeking for his glance in the shades of death. [232]

CHAPTER X

The Shadow Line and 'Typhoon'

AMONG the later works of Conrad, one, *The Shadow Line*, stands out as being both less complex in design and markedly free from all the flaws of lush rhetoric and moralizing which disfigure the others. In this difference from the other works of the same period it resembles 'Typhoon', which was written at the same time as 'Heart of Darkness', *Lord Jim* and 'Falk', but which stands apart from them in its effect in a most striking way.

In 'Typhoon', which was completed in January 1901, we find none of the preoccupation with the 'unforeseen partnership' or the 'other self'; instead, Conrad is hymning the glories of those

> Glad Hearts! without reproach or blot;
> Who do thy work, and know it not.

Captain MacWhirr, with 'just enough imagination to carry him through each successive day, and no more', has indeed considerable resemblance to Hermann in 'Falk', who lacks the imagination to reflect on the implications of the horrors of which he is told. But Captain MacWhirr is told no horrors. The preoccupation with evil, with the shadowy places of human nature, which fills the other stories of this period, is absent here. He is confronted only by a typhoon and by the fighting of the coolies in the labouring ship. To this strain he opposes a 'humane intention and a vague sense of the fitness of things'[233] and by the conviction that:

> There's just so much dirty weather knocking about the world, and the proper thing is to go through it with none of what old Captain Wilson of the *Melita* calls 'storm strategy'.[234]

The implications for him of the phrase 'dirty weather' are wide:

> Had he been informed by an indisputable authority that the end of the world was to be finally accomplished by a catastrophic disturbance of the atmosphere, he would have assimilated the information under the simple idea of dirty weather, and no other, because he had no experience of cataclysms, and belief does not necessarily imply comprehension.[235]

By the end of the story he has a comprehension of a physical cataclysm, but he is not called upon to comprehend anything more. Nothing happens which—in Marlow's words from 'Heart of Darkness'—seems 'to throw a kind of light' on moral or spiritual issues.

By his steadfastness, his perfect ability to meet the test which is imposed on him, he appears to Jukes as 'the frail and resisting voice in his ear, the dwarf sound, unconquered in the giant tumult'.[236] Conrad achieves his effects in this story with a concreteness and an economy of method which contrast strikingly with the rhetoric about ships' captains in *Chance* and *The Rover*, and he succeeds so well just because he is not presenting Captain MacWhirr as the answer to any questions of fundamental good and evil.* He is concerned only with matters where MacWhirr's courage and determination, his 'vague sense of the fitness of things', are adequate.

There is a similar limitation of scope in *The Shadow Line*. The final verdict of the oracular Captain Giles, who, it may be said, seems at first to be stupid, is:

> That's all right ... You will learn soon how not to be faint-hearted. A man has got to learn everything—and that's what so many of these youngsters don't understand ... Yes, that's what it amounts to ... Precious little rest in life for anybody. Better not think of it.[237]

and it is remarkably similar in meaning and in its restriction of application to that of Captain MacWhirr:

> They may say what they like, but the heaviest seas run with the

---

* Dr F. R. Leavis in *The Great Tradition*, 1948, makes a similar point, though in a different context of evaluation, when he sees Captain MacWhirr as being 'without any symbolic portentousness'.

I

wind. Facing it—always facing it—that's the way to get through. You are a young sailor. Face it. That's enough for any man. Keep a cool head.[238]

It is one of the most directly and avowedly autobiographical of Conrad's works*; in the 'Author's Note' it is described as

personal experience seen in perspective with the eye of the mind and coloured by that affection one can't help feeling for such events of one's life as one has no reason to be ashamed of.

He draws on the event in his life of which he also makes use in 'The Secret Sharer' and 'Falk'—his taking over of his first command. The resemblances in detail are numerous: the heavily whiskered first mate and the 'unplayful cub' of a second mate figure in 'The Secret Sharer', the sick seaman Gambril, the dead captain with his empty violin case and his photograph with the 'female in strange draperies' in 'Falk'.

This episode from his past is treated far more simply and straightforwardly than the themes of most of his works—certainly far more than those of the other books of this decade. This outward directness, this absence of 'grouping [sequence] which shifts' and of 'changing lights giving varied effects of perspective',† is a sign of a certain simplicity of aim. The narrator does not in any way stand above the events which he recounts; the book is in this sense far more a naturalistic psychological study than any other important work of Conrad.

We accept as an index of the narrator's state of mind, and as nothing more, such clear-cut moral distinctions as:

But this road my mind's eye could see on a chart, professionally, with all its complications and difficulties, yet simple enough in a way. One is a seaman or one is not.[239]

---

* He even mentions (p. 106) the other occasion when 'in conditions of moral i solation' he kept a diary. We know that this was on the journey into the heart of darkness.

† *V. supra*, p. 3.

In 'Falk' and 'The End of the Tether' a romantic faith in the beauty and courage of life at sea is attacked and undermined; in *Chance* it is elevated to a moral principle capable of offsetting all the evil in the world; here it is seen only as a part of the personality of the narrator at a certain time. There are several passages of reflection by the captain which are strongly reminiscent of some of Marlow's musings on Captain Anthony and his function as captain in *Chance*, but the effect which they make is altogether different.

> A ship [the narrator thinks] My ship! She was mine, more absolutely mine for possession and care than anything in the world; an object of responsibility and devotion. She was there waiting for me, spellbound, unable to move, to live, to get out into the world (till I came), like an enchanted princess . . . I discovered how much of a seaman I was, in heart, in mind, and, as it were, physically—a man exclusively of sea and ships; the sea the only world that counted, and the ships the test of manliness, of temperament, of courage and fidelity—and of love.[240]

There is no question here of pitting this devotion against any such responsibilities and emotions as those evoked by Flora de Barral and her father; here the sea is indeed the only world that counts.

Again, when the narrator says of his ship:

> I knew that, like some rare women, she was one of those creatures whose mere existence is enough to awaken an unselfish delight. One feels that it is good to be in the world in which she has her being,[241]

there is no sense of an absolute judgment on ships or on womankind. This is but a part of the 'ideal completeness of that emotional experience' of getting a first command without the 'preliminary toil and disenchantments of an obscure career'.[242]

Conrad sums up his intention in the book in the 'Author's Note', where he says:

> Primarily the aim of this piece of writing was the presentation of certain facts which certainly were associated with the change from youth, care-free and fervent, to the more self-conscious and more poignant period of maturer life.

As is usual in his work, the narrator is made aware of this change because of the responsibility which faces him in his isolated and central position. There is nothing vague in the story; the clarity of his observation and the precision and brevity with which he displays it are marked features of the story. We see them—together with an astringent touch of humour at the expense of the captain's enchantment with his command—in:

> Right aft two seamen, busy cleaning the steering gear, with the reflected ripples of light running playfully up their bent backs, went on with their work, unaware of me and of the almost affectionate glance I threw at them in passing towards the companion-way of the cabin.[243]

It is a little difficult to understand the viewpoint of the critics of whom he speaks in the 'Author's Note', who saw evidences of the supernatural in the work, for everything is of the most concrete and the shadow line which the narrator must cross is a perfectly natural one.

It is, in fact, when we ask what this shadow line is that we see most clearly the resemblance of this story to 'Typhoon' and its difference from almost all his other works. We have noted the resemblances of detail in 'Falk' and 'The Secret Sharer', but the similarity does not go beyond this. They are also, in their way, accounts of the crossing of shadow lines, the moment of recognition of the undermining presence of the 'other self', of the acceptance of the disturbing reflections about 'the foundation of all the emotions'. But in this work the doubts which assail the captain are reasonable and simple. As in 'Typhoon', Conrad is concerned with situations and problems which can be perfectly dealt with in action; the narrator is concerned only with his fitness to command. The 'seed of everlasting remorse' and the 'sense of guilt' which he feels are due only to his having omitted to examine the contents of the medicine chest before setting sail, and to doubts of his courage.

> I shrink from going on deck to face it [he writes in his diary].

> Now I understand that strange sense of insecurity in my past. I always suspected that I might be no good. And here is proof positive, I am shirking it, I am no good.[244]

But this can be, and is, overcome. He sees it at the end as 'that episode which had been maturing and tempering my character'.[245]

The narrator knows that he has crossed the shadow line when he can say to Captain Giles: 'I am no longer a youngster', and when, in answer to his statement that he is putting out to sea again at once, that oracular figure says: 'You will? . . . That's the way. You'll do'.[246] His courage and readiness to meet an emergency have been proved; the issues with which Conrad is concerned in yet another crossing of a shadow line—that of 'Heart of Darkness'—are not raised.

We can understand, then, why *The Shadow Line* is free from the obvious flaws of the other works of this period. The lush and imprecise rhetoric and the portentous and equally imprecise moralizing, which mar *Lord Jim* and which are predominant features of *Chance* and *Victory* and *The Rover* and *The Arrow of Gold*, are signs of uneasiness and evasion, of an inability to sustain the tension set up by that awareness of corruption and loneliness which give such force to his best work. They are absent here because of the limitation of scope of the story; only a certain range of feelings is brought into activity and this does not include that preoccupation with evil from which, in his later work, Conrad sought refuge.

CHAPTER XI

Self Knowledge

I HAVE already quoted from Conrad's letter to Charles Chassé of 31 January, 1924, in which he protests against the accusation of 'Slavonism':

> That is the truth as far as I know. *Mais après tout vous pouvez avoir raison.* Men have but very little self knowledge, and authors especially are victims of many illusions about themselves.

When we consider the remarks which he makes in letters, in his 'Author's Note' to the Collected Edition and in other occasional writings, we find much to support his view that he may be mistaken. His comment on *Chance*, for example, in a letter to Richard Curle, 14 July, 1923, does not seem true to one's impression of the book:

> Of course there are seamen in a good many of my books. That doesn't make them sea stories any more than the existence of de Barral in *Chance* (and he occupies there as much space as Captain Anthony) makes that novel a story about the financial world.

There is a similar apparent misunderstanding of the balance of a book in his remarks on *The Arrow of Gold* in a letter to S. A. Everitt, 18 February, 1918:

> . . . the novel may be best described as the Study of a Woman . . . It is really an episode related dramatically and in the detailed manner of a study, in that particular life. That it is also an episode in the general experience of the young narrator (the book is written in the first person) serves only to round it off and give it completeness as a novel.

It is certainly not true either that de Barral has an importance in *Chance* approaching that of the highly romanticized Anthony or that the love of Monsieur George—the very centre of the book—merely serves to round off *The Arrow of Gold*.

Nor does it seem that Conrad recognized which were his

best works. There is an interesting letter to J. B. Pinker, written on 10 October, 1907, about negotiations which his agent was conducting with the publishing house of Tauchnitz. Tauchnitz had published his first two volumes, neglected the next seven, and now asked for the tenth. Conrad protests that

> the books that can't be found in the *Collection of British Authors* under Baron Tauchnitz's imprint include the *Nigger*, *Youth*, *Lord Jim*, *Mirror of the Sea*, the very corner stones of my reputation, the best part of seven years of my literary life!

and says that he will not allow Tauchnitz to publish his new work unless he also publishes at least these four as well. Should there be difficulties in the negotiations, however, he suggests: 'Drop the *Nigger* for instance—and be content with 3 books. Or else we could put forward *Nostromo*'. It would seem clear from this that Conrad was not fully aware of the immense power of *Nostromo* and its superiority to his other books.

This is not in itself of much importance, and it is probably true of many writers that they are unaware of what are their best works. Usually, however, they tend for private and personal reasons to overestimate certain of them; in Conrad we find the contrary phenomenon—a constant underestimation of certain aspects of his work and a minimization of some elements in his sensibility. What is most striking is his continued emphasis in his letters on the fact that he is not 'morbid'. In a letter to John Galsworthy of 1908 he makes a number of criticisms of that writer's *Fraternity* (then called *Shadows*) and ends with a postscript:

> I have read and re-read every word, giving due weight to every shade of your meaning, and I still think that the idealization for moral purposes of a man capable of such a spiritual crime is too Tolstoyan to be approved by a plain man without tears and sensibility like myself.

From the context of this remark one can be certain that it is not intended ironically. He had written several letters to

Galsworthy about the work, protesting against the character of Hilary and his rôle in the story ('pure spirits have no use for simple human dignity'), suggesting emendaticns to Galsworthy's plot, and making it quite clear that he is very much in earnest in what he says and that it is against this very matter of 'tears and sensibility' that he is protesting. Yet we can hardly feel that 'a plain man without tears and sensibility' is an adequate description of a man who had written 'Heart of Darkness', *Nostromo*, *Lord Jim* and the other books of his earlier period.

An article by Arthur Symons, written at about the same time, stimulated him to write two letters—one to Edward Garnett and one to Symons himself—in which he speaks in very much the same terms as he does to Galsworthy, but in a far more obviously defensive way.

> I read in a study (still unpublished) of Conrad [he writes to Garnett on 28 August, 1908] that I gloat over scenes of cruelty and am obsessed by visions of spilt blood.
>
> At any rate I have always written with dignity . . . The fact is that I have approached things human in a spirit of piety foreign to those lovers of humanity who would like to make of life a sort of Cook's Personally Conducted Tour—from the cradle to the grave. I have never debased that quasi-religious sentiment by tears and groans and sighs. I have neither grinned nor gnashed my teeth. In a word, I have behaved myself decently—which, except in the gross conventional sense, is not so easy as it looks. Therefore, there are those who reproach me with the pose of brutality, with the lack of all heart, delicacy, sympathy—sentiment—idealism.

The wording of the letter to Symons, written the following day, is almost identical, and goes on:

> It is your penitent beating the floor with his forehead and the ecstatic worshipper at the rails that are obvious to the public eye. The man standing quietly in the shadow of the pillar, if noticed at all, runs the risk of being suspected of sinister designs. Thus I've been called a heartless wretch, a man without ideals and a *poseur* of brutality. But I will confess to you under seal of secrecy that *I don't believe* I am such as I appear to mediocre minds.

He had, a few days previously, written to Symons, thanking

him for the article and condoling with him for having it rejected by an editor, and here again we find the concern to rebut the charge of abnormality:

> I may say that there are certain passages which have surprised me. I did not know that I had 'a heart of darkness' and an 'unlawful' soul. Mr Kurz [*sic*] had, and I have not treated him with the easy nonchalance of an amateur. Believe me, no man paid more for his lines than I have. By that I possess an inalienable right to the use of all my epithets. I did not know that I delighted in cruelty and that the shedding of blood was my obsession.

We may doubtless agree that he was not such as he appeared to 'mediocre minds' and that to describe the shedding of blood as his obsession was foolish, but it is impossible to avoid the conclusion that he is protesting too much. Why, we may ask, this emphasis on 'decent' behaviour, on standing 'quietly in the shadow of the pillar', why this energetic repudiation of 'tears and groans and sighs', of penitence and ecstasy, unless he is uneasy about those aspects of his work of which he is not altogether conscious nor yet totally unaware, and which do not accord with his ideal picture of himself as 'a plain man without tears and sensibility'?

He often presents this contrast in racial terms, in the contrast between the Asiatic and the Western. In the letter to Charles Chassé, from which I quote at the beginning of this chapter, he says:

> The critics detected in me a new note and as, just when I began to write, they had discovered the existence of Russian authors, they stuck that label on me under the name of Slavonism. What I say is that it would have been more just to charge me at most with 'Polonism'. Polish temperament, at any rate, is far removed from Byzantine and Asiatic associations. Poland has absorbed Western ideas, adopted Western culture, sympathized with Western ideals and tendencies as much as it was possible, across the great distances and in the special conditions of its national and political life, whose main task was the struggle for life against Asiatic despotism at its door . . . the formative forces acting on me, at the most plastic and impressionable age, were purely Western; that is French and English. . . . I put

before you my claim to Westernism for no other reason but because I feel myself profoundly in accord with it.

Such a contrast is, however, beside the point; the conflicting elements in Conrad's work cannot be usefully discussed in terms of West and East or of Slavonic and European, but of different kinds of sensibility which are found in both alike.

He seems at times to have been aware that there were elements in his work of which he was not altogether conscious. In the 'Preface' to *The Shorter Tales of Joseph Conrad*, published in *Last Essays*, he writes:

> ... things that 'just happen' in one's work seem impressive and valuable because they spring from sources profounder than the logic of a deliberate theory suggested by acquired learning, let us say, or by lessons drawn from analysed practice.

This—like the letter to Chassé—was written late in his life, but he is in general more aware of these aspects of his work at an earlier period. When Edward Garnett suggested certain alterations to *An Outcast of the Islands*, Conrad replied, on 24 September, 1895:

> Nothing can now unmake my mistake. I shall try—but I shall try without faith, because all my work is produced unconsciously (so to speak) and I cannot meddle to any purpose with what is within myself.—I am sure you understand what I mean.—It isn't in me to improve what has got itself written.

Similarly, on 14 August, 1896, he replies to Garnett's criticisms of 'An Outpost of Progress':

> The construction is bad. It is bad because it was a matter of conscious decision, and I have no discrimination—in the artistic sense. Things get themselves written—and you like them. Things get themselves into shape—and they are tolerable. But when *I* want to write—when *I* do consciously try to write or try to construct, then my ignorance has full play and the quality of my miserable and benighted intelligence is disclosed to the scandalized gaze of my literary father. This is as it should be. I always told you I was a kind of inspired humbug.

Later, he is far more ready to speak as though he has complete control of the creative process and the reservations are rare. We have already seen his description of his 'varied effects of perspective', of the effect aimed at in *The Arrow of Gold*, of his method of isolation. At times he writes as though he can calculate very precisely indeed as to the effects which he will achieve, as in a letter to J. B. Pinker of 18 May, 1907:

> As I've told you my mind runs much on popularity now. I would try to reach it not by sensationalism but by means of taking a widely discussed subject for the *text* of my novel. . . . In short, my idea is to treat those subjects in a novel with a sufficiently interesting story, whose notion has come into my head lately. And, of course, to treat them from a modern point of view.

This lack of complete understanding of his work would not concern us (in that it would be private to Conrad and would not affect our criticism of his books) were it not that after about 1912 he began to achieve an established position as a novelist as well as becoming something in the nature of an elder statesman of the sea. His manuscripts were sought, his comments on his own books canvassed, he toured the United States, contributed critical articles to magazines, wrote a series of 'Author's Notes' to a Collected Edition of his own works and 'Prefaces' to those of other writers. Consequently his attitude towards his own books became widely known and accepted. Nor was he unwilling that this should be so. His claim in a letter to F. N. Double-day of 22 June, 1924, that 'I have never answered any criticism in my life . . . I think that an author who tries to "explain" is exposing himself to a very great risk—the risk of confessing himself a failure', is far from the truth except in so far as he did not engage in public argument with critics and reviewers.

He wrote, for example, to Sir Sidney Colvin on 7 August, 1919, suggesting what he should say about *The Arrow of Gold*, on which the first notices did not please him:

> Perhaps you could also discover a 'personal note of youth 'both in the (so to speak) innocence and the completeness of this love affair—

this emotional adventure fated to end as it ends in a world not meant
for lovers. . . .

When Richard Curle sent him a draft of his review in
The Times Literary Supplement of the whole of the Dent's
Uniform Edition of the Works of Joseph Conrad he made
extensive suggestions in two letters of 14 July and 17 July,
1923, as to how the article should be amended to free him
from 'that infernal tail of ships' and, after speaking at length
of his 'unconventional grouping and perspective' asserted
that:

> . . . this is an opportunity that will never be renewed in my lifetime
> for the judgment of a man who certainly knows my work best and
> not less certainly is known for my closest intimate, but before all is
> the best friend my work has ever had.

He was equally enthusiastic about Curle's *Joseph Conrad:
a Study*,* sympathized with him on its bad reception by
English reviewers and tried in a number of letters to
Alfred A. Knopf to persuade his American publishers to
bring it out. It is therefore worth our while to spend a little
time considering this book as an estimate of Conrad's work
which he was himself anxious to sponsor.

Emphasis throughout is clearly and heavily placed on just
those points which most obscure the finest aspects of
Conrad's work. Curle recognizes that a change has taken
place in the novels in the statement: 'Conrad is both stylist
and artist—but more equally both in his later than in his
earlier work'[247] but is sure that 'there is next to no proof
that his philosophy today is different from what it was
fifteen years ago'.[248] What we have seen as the most
disastrous feature of the later novels—the use of rhetoric to
throw a colouring of romance over such figures as Captain
Anthony and Lena so as to make us accept them at the
author's uncritical valuation—is singled out for praise in
such a typical passage as:

> But to know Conrad's finest figures as they should be known

* 1914.

you must have tasted romance . . . Conrad can impart a wonderful, rich glow to his figures. And in that light they seem close to us, without a word being spoken. Of course, it is another manifestation of atmosphere, but it is not only atmosphere—it is romance as well.[249]

The sections specifically devoted to Conrad's 'philosophy' show most clearly how blind Curle is to the valuable and disturbing features of the early works, and, as I have said, it seems that we can take this as representing Conrad's own blindness. In a comment on 'The End of the Tether', for example, all the 'sinister clearness' of that story is overlooked; instead we are told that:

Captain Whalley's end is, of course, a tragic and terrible end, but there is something so touching and beautiful in the quality of his devotion that it illumines the whole story with the soft atmosphere of triumphant love.[250]

His general conclusions are expressed in tones of indignation and deprecation strikingly like Conrad's own:

I might say that what Conrad admires in character is more or less what every one admires whose mind is not given over to the false casuistry that lies behind so many modern revaluations. He admires courage, compassion, honour, endurance, and in the ordinary interpretation that all sensible persons allow them.[251]

We cannot, of course, assume that Conrad would underwrite every word of Curle's study, but it is abundantly clear that he was anxious that it should be taken as a more or less authoritative introduction to his work. Our conviction that he was unaware of the qualities of his best work and that he tended more and more to encourage a wrong approach to it is therefore confirmed when we find Curle writing:

I feel inclined to say that to his general disillusionment about life there is added an almost naïve belief in goodness . . . we can notice in Conrad, overlaid, as it were, upon his pessimism, the strictest regard for integrity and an austere sense of honour. I do not mean that these things are necessarily antagonistic to a pessimistic conception of life, but I do mean that, in the way Conrad presents them, they might appear old fashioned to stupid persons. For, as I have stated previously, people in England expect original cleverness in their

literary heroes—and expect it, I may add, even concerning the most
straightforward emotions of life. They want mountebanks to tell
them that their integrity is a subject for derision, or that their honour
is, strictly speaking, dishonourable; or else, they want some one who
will for ever be drawing the shades finer and finer. The simplicity
of a man like Conrad, a simplicity hiding an immense subtlety of
perception, is not easily understood.[252]

In fact, the Conrad of the earlier books is as far removed
as possible from a 'naïve belief in goodness' and, if he does
not quite qualify for Curle's definition of a mountebank, he
is certainly—in his reflections on the 'unforeseen partnership', on the 'foundation of all the emotions', on the appeal
of Jim to all sides of Marlow's personality, in the blending
of idealism and corruption in Charles Gould—drawing
the shades very finely.

His repudiation of anything in his work which might
seem to savour of the morbid caused him also to hate any
other writers who appear to him to have this taint. We see
this most strikingly in his comments, in a letter to Edward
Garnett of 27 May, 1912, on Constance Garnett's translation
of Dostoevsky's *The Brothers Karamazov*. After praising the
translation he says of the novel itself:

> It's terrifically bad and impressive and exasperating. Moreover, I
> don't know what D[ostoevsky] stands for or reveals, but I do know
> that he is too Russian for me. It sounds to me like some fierce
> mouthings from prehistoric ages. I understand the Russians have just
> 'discovered' him. I wish them joy.

His hatred of everything Russian—of what he calls 'Slavo-
Tartar Byzantine barbarism'—does not prevent him from
praising at times both Tolstoy and Turgenev, whom
he contrasts with 'Dostoevski, the grimacing, haunted
creature'.[253] It is the result rather, I think, of his rejection
of the qualities which he shares with Dostoevsky. There
are, indeed, very striking resemblances between them.*

---

* Dr Gustav Morf, within the context of his psychoanalytical judgments,
mentions Conrad's hatred as coming from the resemblance of their minds.
Mr T. S. Eliot has linked them, together with Hawthorne and Henry James, as
sharing the same 'essential moral preoccupations' (referred to in F. O. Matthies-
sen's *The Achievement of T. S. Eliot*, p. 23).

The debt in *Under Western Eyes* to the Russian novelist is clear and is chiefly to *The Possessed*, but the full resemblance goes much deeper. There are a number of very close similarities in the way in which they enforce their judgments and conclusions as well as in these judgments and conclusions themselves. The element of 'sordid farce' as a manifestation of evil is common to them both and the perception of 'double motives'—of such importance in Myshkin's view of human nature in *The Idiot* and elsewhere in Dostoevsky's novels—is closely akin to Conrad's preoccupation with the sources of our idealistic feelings in such works as 'Falk' and *Nostromo*. The greatest resemblance, however—and it lies at the heart of the best work of them both—is the recurrent situation of the obviously 'good' man who is confronted by a 'double' whom he cannot repudiate and who makes him aware of evil or equivocal qualities in himself which he would rather not see. The link in *Crime and Punishment* is between Raskolnikov and Svidrigailov, in *The Brothers Karamazov* between Ivan Karamazov and Smerdyakov, in *The Possessed* (though here the matter is more complicated) between Stavrogin and Pyotr Stepanovitch Verhovensky. In Conrad we have the undeniable connections between Lord Jim and Gentleman Brown and between Jim and Marlow, between Marlow and Kurtz, between the narrator of 'The Secret Sharer' and Leggatt.

It seems certain that Conrad attacked Dostoevsky so violently, not because they were temperamentally dissimilar, but because Dostoevsky keeps always in the forefront of his work elements similar to those in Conrad's sensibility which he had thrust to the back and any suggestion of which he repudiated. If we seek a writer with whom we can profitably compare Conrad we shall choose Dostoevsky and not, as Richard Curle suggests—presumably with Conrad's approval—Flaubert or Turgenev.

But a misunderstanding about a writer, once born, is hard to kill and harder still if it has the writer himself as godfather. Conrad was anxious to escape from the stupid misunderstandings which tied nautical or Slavonic labels on his books, but his unawareness of his finest qualities have probably been more of a hindrance to a true appreciation of his work even than these. He would doubtless have been pleased had he known how often his words from the 'Familiar Preface' to *A Personal Record* would be quoted as a key to his work:

> Those who read me know my conviction that the world, the temporal world, rests on a few very simple ideas: so simple that they must be as old as the hills. It rests, notably, among others, on the idea of Fidelity.

Yet, as we have seen, there is a great deal more in his novels and stories than such a statement would suggest, and he is a greater novelist because of it.

CHAPTER XII

Conclusion (1975)

In a chronological study of a writer who, like Conrad, did his best work comparatively early, we may be left with a sense of disappointment. Such a feeling should be dissipated when we reflect that, though his reputation rests upon part only of his output, it is not a particularly small part—certainly not less than four novels and rather more tales of varying length. Not many English novelists can claim more. The only point of noting a decline is to emphasise what he declined from.

His work is remarkably varied; the books between 'Youth' and *The Secret Agent* manifest a restless exploratory energy. But they share, as I have suggested, an individual vision, a cast of mind, which confronts us, upsettingly, with certain repeated situations. Conrad's concern is with a powerful sense of potential weakness and betrayal lurking under an apparent confidence in an established code of behaviour and waiting for the right circumstances of stress to emerge, often with devastating power. His technical method of isolating his characters enables him to project these states of mind very forcefully through objects and circumstances which are both physical, natural, inevitably imposed by the real world, and at the same time symbolic of the plight of the characters.

To put matters thus may suggest that Conrad is essentially a systematic metaphysical thinker. This seemes to me to be inaccurate. Certainly he employed large quasi-metaphysical terms, especially in his least successfully rhetorical moments, and he speaks of human behaviour roundly in terms of good and evil. Certainly, too, he encountered at second and third and fourth (and occasionally perhaps even at first) hand metaphysical doctrines which were being discussed at the time, and we can sometimes trace echoes of them in his work. But this is a very different matter from being a systematic metaphysical thinker, and attempts to present him as a Schopenhauerian, for example (Schopenhauer is the favourite candidate at the moment), seem misguided. There are, of course, occasions when, rather unconvincingly, he offers general statements as if he believes that they encapsulate meanings. The Marlow of *Chance* is given to this indulgence, but so, more damagingly because the novel has more in it to be damaged, does the Marlow of *Lord Jim*. But when he is writing at the height of his powers Conrad's individual vision is presented in a remarkably complex and often indirect manner, involving not only such basic fictional methods as engaging our sympathies, often surprisingly, with his characters and generating suspense and resolving it, but also shifts of tone and disconcerting juxtapositions of happenings. When we harden this dense and complex effect into doctrines it is often because of a tendency to support our view by what seem appropriate quotations. We inevitably tend to rely on those utterances which can be taken as general statements. The amount of weight which has been placed, for example, on Stein's famous comment on the destructive element seems to me to be out of all proportion to the significance of the passage in its context. It is one among many remarks made by Stein, the effect of all of which is to create a mood in which to think about Jim and not a series of formulations by which to measure him.

What lies at the heart of Conrad's work is surely not metaphysics but politics—politics understood in the widest sense. Much of private life—sexual relationships, family, neighbourly friendships, domestic rhythms—is of little interest to him, and when he writes about such matters, as in *Chance* and *Victory*, he displays his weaknesses rather than his strengths. His interest lies in the interplay of groups, the conflict between personal feelings and professional duties; he sees men as fulfilling public roles as well as leading private lives and he focusses attention upon their shared efforts and their conflicts of interest. Few novelists have written so much about work as Conrad, though the fact that the work is so often that of ship-handling—an exotic task for most readers —has tended to make us overlook the fact. But his tales of the sea are essentially about what we might call the politics of shipboard life. Even so apparently private a study of self-doubt as 'The Secret Sharer' gains its force from the narrator's awareness of professional responsibilities and his relationship with the crew over whom he has power but whose judgements he cannot ignore. It seems natural that Lord Jim should seek to redeem his loss of professional honour by becoming a Grand Vizier. The captain in *The Shadow Line* says of himself: 'In that community I stood, like a king in his country, in a class all by myself. I mean an hereditary king, not a mere elected head of state.' The political image is appropriate; he has to make a group of men work together and the skills which he must use are political ones—example, appeal, command. In 'Youth' and *The Nigger of the 'Narcissus'*, though neither is told so completely from the point of view of command, the same group relationships and the same problems of organization are described.

There is, however, one characteristic of these stories which distinguishes them from the strictly political novels, *Nostromo*, *The Secret Agent* and *Under Western Eyes*; in them at least one limited aim is clear and unquestionable—to navigate the ship and to preserve life at sea. The isolation of the situation concentrates the problems and convincingly limits them; Conrad does not have to consider such matters as the economic issues of the trade in which they are engaged nor the morality of sending men to sea in leaky ships. He tells us in 'Youth' that the owner of the *Judea* went bankrupt, that 'the owner, the underwriters, and the charterers squabbled amongst themselves' and makes comic play with Captain Beard's injunction to save what they can 'for the underwriters' when they abandon ship; but we are told this by a man for whom it has no real significance. What, in *The Shadow Line*, he calls 'silly commercial complications' are avoided. Nothing is allowed to question the simplicity of the immediate task—as, indeed, nothing would in real life. It is interesting to observe in 'Heart of Darkness', where the morality of the trading is an issue and therefore the purpose of the voyage, that even though Marlow speaks of the therapeutic value of getting his ungainly steamboat to work he comes back down the river ill, a passenger and not a commander.

The pessimism of the sea stories is thus modified because Conrad's positive values, a belief in doing one's job properly, in fairness, in courage, in the stoic acceptance of blows, have a real, if limited, value. His protagonists may find themselves thrust into situations where the code by which they regulate their conduct seems precarious, unlikely to defend them against all the forces which may be arrayed against them, but at least in the situations which immediately confront them their duty is clear and they can win a limited victory.

In the overtly political novels there is no such unquestioned aim. There may be actions in which the practical virtues remain unquestionable but they are subsumed under larger themes where the end cannot claim legitimacy. Conrad's political view is one of gloomy scepticism, spiced with the sardonic humour of one who watches the futility of all political effort. There is no legitimate authority and no sense of political development nor of broadly based political movements. In *Under Western Eyes* the Russian state is a tyranny, but the revolutionaries are idealistic or eccentric freaks. In *The Secret Agent* Vladimir's state is barbarous but Sir Ethelred and Toodles inspire no more than amiable contempt; the anarchists are shams, except for the Professor who is disinterested but fanatically destructive.

It seems likely that this sceptical and despairing view

originated in Conrad's Polish origins. I am not so much concerned with his specifically personal circumstances, with his guardian uncle's view that his father's revolutionary plans were futile and even harmful, and with the conflict between the outlook of the Bobrowski and the Korzeniow-ski families. These must certainly have played some part but there is no need to base conclusions on the inevitably shaky ground of biography. We need only reflect on the pressures to which any member of the Polish landowning class would have been subjected under Russian rule. For that matter, things would not have seemed very different if Conrad had been born a Croat in Hungary under the Habsburgs or a thoughtful Galician. In any such case he would have felt, as no English writer of the period could have done, what it was to be a puppet (whether rebellious or complaisant) in a state whose legitimacy was dubious to all but the blind or selfish, and yet to see little hope of progressive change and none whatever with which he could sympathize.

Such an attitude is in many ways by definition conserva-tive. Who would hazard what little order and comfort and justice we have by attempts at change in which we do not believe? Better Sir Edward than what may take his place. This nihilist conservatism, combined with the assent which Conrad necessarily gives to the authority of, say, Captain Allistoun and thus the rather easy contempt which lashes Donkin, is responsible for our sense that at bottom Conrad sympathises with authority. But in truth his scepticism is more corrosive than we may think; attempts to change society may be futile but authority has no moral force. Nowhere is this more clearly shown than in Winnie Verloc's attempt to explain to Stevie the function of the police. He, in his pity for the cabman and his horse, has formulated his judgement as 'Bad world for poor people' and invokes the police as agents for righting wrongs—'He had formed for himself an ideal conception of the metro-politan police as a sort of benevolent institution for the suppression of evil'. Winnie feels the need to put him right and she also knows that the word 'steal' upsets him; she chooses, therefore, a formula upon which the Professor could hardly improve: 'They are there so that them as have nothing shouldn't take anything away from them who have.'

This view of politics—one which has no faith in the legitimacy of established order but also no faith in progress through political development and which sees men as almost inevitably corrupted by the public roles which they have to play—finds expression most fully in Conrad's masterpiece, *Nostromo*. The political analysis is founded upon political fact; we know that Conrad, aided by his friend Cunninghame Graham, studied South American history (though he tended to conceal the fact and allow people to think he made it all up) and this emerges throughout. But the analyst's mood is rooted in the disillusions of Eastern Europe.

But if *Nostromo* is, as many believe, the best political novel in the language this is not just because of the shrewdness of its analysis of the exploitation of an underdeveloped country by the invested capital of the 'Anglo-Saxon' powers, but rather because the complex form of the book does justice to the double vision of men and women as both individuals and as socially determined beings. The very frustrations which this arouses in the reader serve the meaning of the book.

In all substantial novels there is an inherent tension between our perception of form, of controlling structure, and our interest in the characters as individuals. In *Nostromo* this tension is very powerful; there are many elements in the book which are potentially or actually frustrating or irksome but to which, in the long run, we give our assent. The tension thus set up is in effect a political statement.

This is seen in its most elementary form even in the way in which the individuals are referred to in terms of their public roles—the Capataz, the President-Dictator, the Gobernador, the Señor Administrador, and, most significantly, in the

name given by the Europeans (complete, we are told, with
Mitchell's mispronunciation) to the eponymous hero,
Nostromo, 'our man'. I think it is true that at first reading
this labelling by function is found either slightly muddling
or slightly mannered. It is a small but valuable part of the
book's effect that we should feel this enough to be conscious
of our later recognition that, for example, the individuality
of Gian' Battista Fidanza is swallowed up for some in his
role as the Capataz de Cargadores—and to some extent it is
swallowed up for him, too—and that for the Europeans he,
like so many of the other characters, is simply 'our man'.
In the particular case of Nostromo we are pointed to this
conclusion by the Padrona, a shrewd political analyst.*

It is, of course, by the omnipresent symbolism of the silver
of the mine, with which is linked the legend of the treasure
seekers of Azuera, that the political judgement of the book is
most enforced. There are times when this, too, may seem
overdone, when its predetermining power constrains the
characters' freedom so that they are perilously close to
seeming puppets. As one gets to know the book better one
realises that they are, indeed, puppets, but not those of a
puppet-master novelist so much as of a political situation
whose central controlling symbol seems not imposed by the
writer but elucidated by him from the facts of the situation.

The structure, with its great use of time-shifts and changes
of viewpoint, also functions to show the futility of the
struggles of individuals within a political and economic

---

* I am aware that in speaking thus of our being muddled or irked I may be
thought to take an unduly simple view. The practised reader, it may be said, is not
so easily put out and critics should write of the mature response which comes
when we know the book well and have put all muddle behind us. This is, I am sure,
a great mistake. Certain very simple initial reactions should, if we read properly,
remain alive in our response even after we have developed more sophisticated
ones. An awareness of how we have modified our judgements on subsequent
readings is an important part of our final response. This is true of any book but it
is particularly so of *Nostromo* since these modifications, these revaluations of
significance, are central to the meaning of the book. In *The Approach to Fiction:
Good and Bad Readings of Novels* (1972) I discuss at greater length the consequences
of a novel's dual existence as both a created object on which we look back and an
experience which we undergo.

situation which dwarfs them. The book's method is to plunge us into situations where we feel for characters faced by danger or the need to make decisions and then, without comment, to see these personal predicaments as part of a process which diminishes them. Thus Decoud's letter to his sister, nearly half way through the book, sets out in the context of his plans for defeating the revolution and setting up an independent province those happenings which we have seen, muddled and fragmentary, in the early chapters. More strikingly, the jump forward in time to Captain Mitchell's boring reminiscences gives us as history what we had been preparing to respond to as personal victory or disaster. The novel, one might say, exemplifies the process whereby a multiplicity of personal experiences becomes, in retrospect, the generalised 'Fifty Years of Misrule'.

Nostromo does not merely express a political attitude; it embodies it, in the sense that the process by which the reader comes to understand it, changing his viewpoint and coming to terms with certain muddles and disappointments, is the political statement itself. It is this, above all, which gives the novel its extraordinary impression of density, solidity, which can only come from a large theme which finds its appropriate form. Maturity of outlook and originality of technique are perfectly matched. Had Conrad written nothing else his place would be assured. When we add to it 'Heart of Darkness', *The Secret Agent*, *Lord Jim* and half a dozen other works we recognize a body of work which makes all but a handful of other English novelists look superficial.

APPENDIX I

Notes

1 *Lord Jim: A Tale* 1900, p. 387 (page numbers throughout are from the Uniform Edition of J. M. Dent & Sons, Ltd.)
2 *Nostromo: A Tale of the Seaboard*, pp. 36–7
3 ibid., p. 146
4 ibid., p. 37
5 ibid., p. 261
   1904, pp. 36–7
6 op. cit., p. 503
7 *Youth: A Narrative; and Two Other Stories*. 1902, p. 51
8 *Last Essays*, 1926, p. 25
9 op. cit., p. 106
10 ibid., p. 52
11 ibid., pp. 60–1
12 ibid., p. 61
13 ibid., pp. 61–2
14 ibid., p. 75
15 ibid., p. 68
16 ibid., p. 70
17 ibid., pp. 50–1
18 ibid., p. 85
19 ibid., p. 96
20 ibid., p. 99
21 ibid., p. 131
22 ibid., p. 138
23 ibid., pp. 141–2
24 ibid., p. 144
25 ibid., p. 159
26 ibid., p. 147
27 ibid., pp. 150–1
28 ibid., p. 152
29 ibid., p. 162
30 op. cit., pp. 36–7
31 op. cit., p. 30
32 op. cit., p. 187
33 ibid., p. 212
34 ibid., p. 271
35 ibid., p. 288
36 ibid., p. 215
37 ibid., p. 289
38 ibid., p. 300
39 ibid., p. 251
40 ibid., p. 293
41 ibid., p. 319
42 ibid., p. 324
43 ibid., p. 324
44 op. cit., p. 50
45 ibid., p. 121
46 ibid., p. 226
47 ibid., pp. 352–3
48 ibid., p. 387
49 ibid., p. 391
50 ibid., p. 394
51 ibid., p. 148
52 ibid., 416
53 ibid., p. 51
54 ibid., pp. 179–80
55 ibid., p. 93
56 ibid., p. 50
57 ibid., p. 131
58 ibid., p. 43
59 ibid., pp. 43–4
60 ibid., p. 68
61 ibid., p. 59
62 ibid., p. 93
63 ibid., pp. 320–1
64 *Typhoon, and Other Stories*, 1903, p. 195
65 ibid., p. 194
66 ibid., p. 152
67 ibid., p. 200
68 ibid., p. 234
69 ibid., p. 223
70 ibid., p. 149
71 ibid., p. 156
72 ibid., pp. 223–4
73 op. cit., p. 249
74 op. cit., pp. 214–15
75 op. cit., p. 76
76 ibid., p. 77
77 ibid., p. 9
78 ibid., p. 554
79 ibid., p. 131
80 ibid., p. 502
81 ibid., p. 503
82 ibid., Part II, Chapter IV, pp. 164–72

83 op. cit., p. 107
84 ibid., p. 5
85 ibid., p. 259
86 ibid., p. 501
87 ibid., p. 526
88 ibid., p. 521
89 ibid., p. 561
90 ibid., p. 400
91 ibid., p. 460
92 ibid., p. 259
93 ibid., p. 364
94 ibid., p. 398
95 ibid., p. 66
96 ibid., p. 64
97 ibid., pp. 214–15
98 ibid., p. 245
99 ibid., p. 379
100 ibid., pp. 406–7
101 ibid., p. 408
102 ibid., p. 503
103 ibid., p. 511
104 ibid., p. 522
105 ibid., p. 59
106 loc. cit.
107 ibid., p. 557
108 ibid., p. 189
109 ibid., p. 218
110 ibid., p. 318
111 ibid., p. 438
112 loc. cit.
113 ibid., p. 561
114 ibid., p. 431
115 ibid., p. 504
116 ibid., p. 36
117 ibid., p. 473. All quotations in this section are from Part III, Chapter X, pp. 473–489
118 *'Twixt Land and Sea: Tales*, 1912, p. 113
119 ibid., p. 95
120 ibid., p. 96
121 ibid., p. 110
122 ibid., p. 99
123 ibid., p. 100
124 ibid., p. 102
125 loc. cit.
126 ibid., p. 119
127 ibid., p. 120
128 loc. cit.
129 ibid., p. 110
130 ibid., p. 125
131 ibid., pp. 113–14
132 ibid., p. 129
133 ibid., p. 130
134 ibid., p. 139
135 ibid., p. 135
136 ibid., p. 142
137 ibid., p. 143
138 ibid., p. 96
139 *Under Western Eyes*, 1911, p. 25
140 ibid., p. 67
141 ibid., p. 66
142 ibid., p. 163
143 ibid., p. 293
144 ibid., p. 345
145 ibid., p. 60
146 ibid., p. 175
147 ibid., p. 381
148 first mentioned p. 135
149 ibid., p. 255
150 ibid., p. 196
151 *The Secret Agent: A Simple Tale*, 1907, p. 6
152 ibid., pp. 12–13
153 ibid., pp. 13–14
154 ibid., p. 50
155 ibid., p. 46
156 ibid., pp. 92–3
157 ibid., p. 93
158 ibid., p. 122
159 ibid., p. 97
160 ibid., p. 114
161 ibid., p. 106
162 ibid., p. 139
163 *Chance: A Tale in Two Parts*, 1913, p. 429
164 ibid., p. 116
165 ibid., p. 312
166 ibid., p. 331
167 ibid., p. 326
168 ibid., p. 333
169 ibid., p. 346
170 ibid., p. 416
171 ibid., p. 328
172 ibid., pp. 328–9
173 ibid., p. 212
174 ibid., p. 223
175 ibid., p. 230
176 ibid., p. 231
177 ibid., p. 238
178 ibid., pp. 426–7
179 ibid., p. 325
180 ibid., p. 162
181 ibid., p. 352
182 ibid., p. 329
183 Part II, Chapter VI, pp. 422–35
184 'The New Novel' from *Notes on Novelists*, 1914.

185 op. cit., p. 103
186 ibid., p. 353
187 ibid., p. 126
188 ibid., p. 442
189 ibid., p. 353
190 ibid., p. 311
191 ibid., p. 310
192 ibid., p. 150
193 ibid., p. 288
194 ibid., p. 32–3
195 ibid., pp. 309–10
196 ibid., p. 321
197 *Victory: An Island Tale*, 1915, p. 349
198 ibid., p. 393
199 ibid., p. 379
200 ibid., p. 245
201 ibid., p. 406
202 ibid., p. 410
203 ibid., p. 27
204 ibid., p. 106
205 ibid., p. 13
206 loc. cit.
207 ibid., p. 18
208 ibid., p. 51
209 ibid., p. 66
210 ibid., p. 65
211 ibid., p. 90
212 op. cit., p. 175
213 ibid., p. 325
214 ibid., pp. 198–9
215 ibid., pp. 115–16
216 ibid., p. 329
217 ibid., p. 285
218 ibid., p. 378
219 ibid., p. 382
220 ibid., p. 389
221 ibid., p. 104
222 ibid., p. 113
223 ibid., p. 288
224 ibid., p. 149
225 ibid., p. 231
226 ibid., p. 152
227 ibid., p. 396
228 ibid., p. 88
229 ibid., p. 399
230 ibid., p. 404
231 ibid., p. 406
232 ibid., p. 407
233 op. cit., p. 85
234 ibid., p. 34
235 ibid., p. 20
236 ibid., p. 47
237 *The Shadow Line: A Confession*, 1916, p. 132
238 op. cit., p. 34.
239 op. cit., p. 44
240 ibid., p. 40
241 ibid., p. 49
242 ibid., p. 50
243 ibid., pp. 50–51
244 ibid., p. 107
245 ibid., p. 129
246 ibid., p. 132
247 op. cit., p. 220
248 ibid., p. 165
249 ibid., p. 110
250 ibid., p. 114
251 ibid., pp. 104–5
252 ibid., p. 90
253 The phrase occurs in a letter of May, 1917, to Edward Garnett
254 In the essay 'Modern Fiction' in *The Common Reader* (First Series)

APPENDIX II

The Works of Joseph Conrad

This list is arranged chronologically in order of composition and not of publication. The dates given are those on which the works were completed. Most of the information upon which they are based comes from Conrad's letters. The titles of short stories are in roman type, those of complete works are in italics; this method of reference has been followed in the text of this study.

'The Black Mate'	g	1886	?
Almayer's Folly: A Story of an Eastern River		1894	May
An Outcast of the Islands		1895	September
'The Idiots'	a	1896	May
'The Outpost of Progress'	a	1896	July
'The Lagoon'	a	1896	August?
'The Return'	a	1896	Summer
The Nigger of the 'Narcissus': A Tale of the Sea		1897	February
'Karain, a Memory'	a	1897	February
'Youth'	b	1898	May–June
'Heart of Darkness'	b	1899	Jan.–February
Lord Jim: A Tale		1900	July
'Typhoon'	c	1901	January
'Falk'	c	1901	May
'Amy Foster'	c	1901	June
'The End of the Tether'	b	1902	October
†'Tomorrow'	c		
Nostromo: A Tale of the Seaboard		1904	September
'The Brute'	d	1905	Summer
'Gaspar Ruiz'	d	1905	November
'An Anarchist'	d	1905	November
'The Informer'	d	1905	December
The Mirror of the Sea: Memories and Impressions		1906	April
The Secret Agent: A Simple Tale		1906	September ?
'The Duel'	d	1907	January
'Il Conde'	d	1907	late
A Personal Record		1908	Autumn
'The Secret Sharer'	e	1909	November
Under Western Eyes		1910	January
'A Smile of Fortune'	e	1910	August
'The Partner'	f	1910	Summer
'Freya of the Seven Isles'	e	1910	Summer
'Prince Roman'	g	1911	
Chance: A Tale in Two Parts		1912	March

† I can find no record of the date of composition of this story.

'The Inn of the Two Witches'	*f*	1912	early
'Because of the Dollars'	*f*	1912	early
'The Planter of Malata'	*f*	1913	late
Victory: An Island Tale		1914	June
The Shadow Line: A Confession		1915	March
'The Warrior's Soul'	*g*	1916	early
'The Tale'	*g*	1916	early
The Arrow of Gold: A Story between Two Notes		1918	June
The Rescue: A Romance of the Shallows		1919	May
The Rover		1922	July
Suspense: A Napoleonic Novel	(Unfinished: published posthumously)		

a	signifies published in	*Tales of Unrest*, 1898	
b	,,	*Youth: A Narrative; and Two Other Stories*, 1902	
c	,,	*Typhoon, and Other Stories*, 1903	
d	,,	*A Set of Six*, 1908	
e	,,	*'Twixt Land and Sea: Tales*, 1912	
f	,,	*Within the Tides: Tales*, 1915	
g	,,	*Tales of Hearsay*, 1925	

INDEX